PLANNING GUIDE

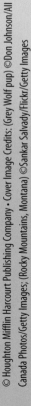
C2016 Edition

Copyright © by Houghton Mifflin Harcourt Publishing Company

Printed in the U.S.A.

ISBN 978-0-544-71206-5

2 3 4 5 6 7 8 9 10   0607   24 23 22 21 20 19 18 17 16 15

4500570804   ^ B C D E F G

Table of Contents

© Houghton Mifflin Harcourt Publishing Company • Image Credits: (bc) ©Peter Dazeley/Photographer's Choice RF/Getty Images

END-OF-YEAR RESOURCES

Review Projects

Getting Ready for Grade 2

These lessons review prerequisite skills and prepare for next year's content.

Correlations

It's Effective and Accessible Math

GO Math! for Kindergarten–Grade 6 combines powerful teaching strategies with never-before-seen components, to offer everything needed to successfully build a strong foundation in elementary math skills and concepts.

VOLUME 1

Operations and Algebraic Thinking

Big Idea Develop a conceptual understanding of concepts and strategies for addition and subtraction.

© Houghton Mifflin Harcourt Publishing Company

Big Idea

GO DIGITAL

Go online! Your math lessons are interactive. Use iTools, Animated Math Models, the Multimedia eGlossary, and more.

Chapter 1 Overview

In this chapter, you will explore and discover answers to the following **Essential Questions**:

- How can you model adding within 10?
- How do you show adding to a group?
- How do you model putting together?
- How do you show adding in any order?

Chapter 2 Overview

In this chapter, you will explore and discover answers to the following **Essential Questions**:

- How can you subtract numbers from 10 or less?
- How do you model taking apart?
- How do you show taking from a group?
- How do you subtract to compare?

Personal Math Trainer
Online Assessment and Intervention

v

perfect for 21st century students.

GO Math! gets students engaged with learning, focused on working smarter, and ready for the future. The Interactive Student Edition offers the unique Personal Math Trainer® Powered by Knewton™—a state of the art online, and adaptive, assessment, and intervention system. In this tablet-based, mobile, and online environment, students receive a completely personalized learning experience, focused on in-depth understanding, fluency, and application of standards.

A way of thinking about learning,

GO Math! helps students engage with content and the mathematical processes in new ways. Lessons begin with problem-based situations and then build to more abstract problems. All along the way, students use multiple models, manipulatives, quick pictures, and symbols to build mathematical understandings. And, best of all, **GO Math!** is write-in at every grade level, so students are completely engaged.

GO Math! practice, homework, and review pages are included in the Student Edition!

that truly prepares students for High-Stakes Assessments.

GO Math! works! Using manipulatives, multiple models, and rich, rigorous questions, students move through a carefully sequenced arc of learning where they develop deep conceptual understanding, and then practice, apply, and discuss what they know with skill and confidence.

An online teacher tool offering the functionality of a planner...

GO Math! helps with the big jobs of teaching. Using the Teacher Dashboard and Smart Planner, teachers create lesson plans and access great resources that can be sequenced to align with district requirements or classroom needs. There's more. The *GO Math!* technology and classroom instruction work together. Students alternate often between engaging with their teacher and classmates and focusing on online content personalized to their learning pace and progress.

Math on the Spot videos, available for every lesson in *GO Math!*, support teachers and students, within the classroom and at home.

There are 14 sheep in the flock.
5 sheep run away.
How many sheep are left?

Subtract 4 to get to 10

with the convenience of mobile.

Access to all of these great resources is right at your finger tips, saving you valuable planning and teaching time.

Create daily lesson plans with a single search.

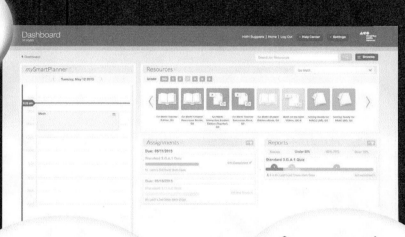

Organize resources quickly.

See a snapshot of recent student report data.

Grab-and-Go Resources,

GO Math! works for the busy teacher. Everything from Teacher Editions to activity centers to manipulatives are organized in a ready-made, grab-and-go way to save you time.

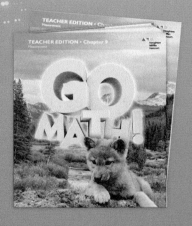

GO Math! Teacher Editions are color-coded by Big Idea and organized by chapters to help teachers quickly identify materials and flexibly organize their curriculum. And instruction is organized around the 5 Es—Engage, Explore, Explain, Elaborate, and Evaluate. With this approach, **GO Math!** emphasizes in-depth understanding and communication within an engaging, inclusive classroom environment.

perfect for the busy teacher.

The *Grab-and-Go!™ Differentiated Centers Kits* are ready-made, differentiated math centers with activities, games, and literature. Resources for every lesson and special challenge materials make the *Grab-and-Go!™ Differentiated Centers Kits* the perfect resource for independent practice.

Digital Resources

FOR LEARNING...

 Interactive Student Edition

- Immerses students in an interactive, multi-sensory math environment
- Enhances learning with scaffolded, interactive instruction and just-in-time feedback
- Provides audio reinforcement for each lesson
- Makes learning a two-way experience, using a variety of interactive tools

FOR ASSESSMENT AND INTERVENTION...

 Personal Math Trainer

- Creates a personalized learning path for each student
- Provides opportunities for practice, homework, and assessment
- Includes worked-out examples and helpful video support
- Offers targeted intervention and extra support to build proficiency and understanding

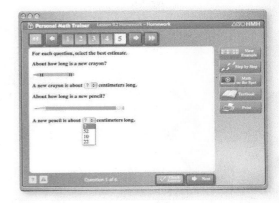

FOR DAILY MATH TUTORING...

 Math on the Spot Videos

- Models good problem-solving thinking in every lesson
- Engages students through interesting animations and fun characters
- Builds student problem-solving proficiency and confidence
- Builds the skills needed for success on high-stakes assessments

FOR TEACHING...

 Interactive Teacher Digital Management Center

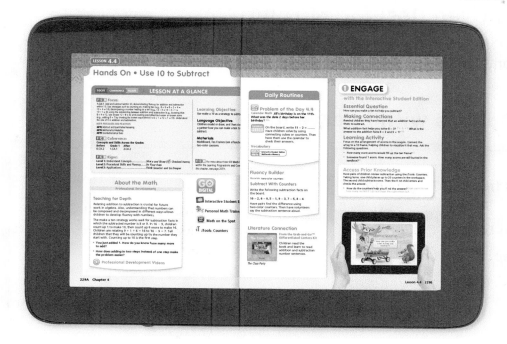

Teacher Edition

- Plan your lessons from the convenience of your classroom, at home, or on the go
- View student lessons 24/7
- Access *Math on the Spot* videos anytime, anywhere
- Offers learning and instructional activities and suggestions

Professional Development Videos

- Learn more about the content
- See first-hand the integration of the Math Processes and Practices
- Watch students engaged in a productive struggle

DIGITAL RESOURCE...
Digital Management System

- Manage online all program content and components
- Search for and select resources
- Identify resources based on student ability and needs
- View and assign student lessons, practice, assessments, and more

Assessment ➡ Diagnosis ➡ Intervention

Data-Driven Decision Making

Go Math! allows for quick and accurate data-driven decision making so you can spend more instructional time tailored to children's needs.

Program Assessment Options with Intervention

Diagnostic

To allow children to be engaged from the beginning of the year

- **Prerequisite Skills Inventory** in *Chapter Resources*
- **Beginning-of-Year Test** in *Chapter Resources*
- **Show What You Know** in *Student Edition*

- Intensive Intervention
- Intensive Intervention User Guide
- Strategic Intervention
- Personal Math Trainer

Formative

To monitor children's understanding of lessons and to adjust instruction accordingly

- **Lesson Quick Check** in *Teacher Edition*
- **Lesson Practice** in *Student Edition*
- **Mid-Chapter Checkpoint** in *Student Edition*
- **Portfolio** in *Chapter Resources and Teacher Edition*
- **Middle-of-Year Test** in *Chapter Resources*

- **Reteach** with each lesson
- **RtI: Tier 1 and Tier 2 Activities** online
- Personal Math Trainer

Summative

To determine whether children have achieved the chapter objectives

- **Chapter Review/Test** in *Student Edition*
- **Chapter Test** in *Chapter Resources* (high-stakes assessment formats)
- **Performance Assessment Task** in *Chapter Resources*
- **End-of-Year Test** in *Chapter Resources*
- **Getting Ready for Grade 2 Test** in *Getting Ready Lessons and Resources*

- **Reteach** with each lesson
- **RtI: Tier 1 and Tier 2 Activities** online
- Personal Math Trainer

Tracking Yearly Progress

Beginning of the Year

The Beginning-of-Year Test determines how many of this year's important concepts children already understand. Adjust lesson pacing for skills that need light coverage and allow more time for skills children find challenging.

During the Year

Chapter Tests, Performance Tasks, and the Middle-of-Year Test monitor children's progress throughout the year. Plan time to reinforce skills children have not mastered.

End of the Year

The End-of-Year Test assesses children's mastery of this year's important concepts. Reinforce skills that children find challenging in order to provide the greatest possible success.

Performance Assessment

Performance Assessment helps to reveal the thinking strategies children use to solve problems. The Performance Tasks in *GO Math!* can be used to complete the picture for how children reason about mathematics.

GO Math! has a Performance Task for each Chapter and each Big Idea. Each assessment has several tasks that target specific math concepts, skills, and strategies. These tasks can help assess children's ability to use what they have learned to solve everyday problems. Teachers can plan for children to complete one task at a time or use an extended amount of time to complete the entire assessment. Projects for each Big Idea also serve to assess children's problem solving strategies and understanding of mathematical concepts they learn in the Big Idea.

The Performance Tasks and Big Idea Projects offer the following features:

- They model good instruction.
- They are diagnostic.
- They encourage the thinking process.
- They are flexible.
- They use authentic instruction.
- They are scored holistically.

GO Math! also has optional Diagnostic Interview Assessment at the beginning of each chapter to help determine each child's readiness for the content in the chapter. The Diagnostic Interview assesses children at the concrete or pictorial level. Intervention options are provided.

 ## GO Math! Personal Math Trainer

- HTML5-based online homework, assessment, and intervention engine
- Pre-built online homework, tests, and intervention (with Personal Study Plans)
- Algorithmic, tech-enhanced items, with wrong answer feedback, and learning aids

Authors

Edward B. Burger, Ph.D.
President, Southwestern University
Georgetown, Texas

Juli K. Dixon, Ph.D.
Professor, Mathematics Education
University of Central Florida
Orlando, Florida

Matthew R. Larson, Ph.D.
K-12 Curriculum Specialist for Mathematics
Lincoln Public Schools
Lincoln, Nebraska

Martha E. Sandoval-Martinez
Math Instructor
El Camino College
Torrance, California

Steven J. Leinwand
Principal Research Analyst
American Institutes for Research (AIR)
Washington, D.C.

Contributor and Consultant

Rena Petrello
Professor, Mathematics
Moorpark College
Moorpark, CA

Elizabeth Jiménez
CEO, GEMAS Consulting
Professional Expert on English Learner Education
Bilingual Education and Dual Language
Pomona, California

Go Math! Reviewers and Field Test Teachers

Janine L. Ambrose
Instructional Coach
Grades Taught: K–7
Sunset Ridge Elementary
Pendergast Elementary School District
Phoenix, Arizona

Patricia R. Barbour
Teacher: Grade 2
Sara Lindemuth Primary School
Susquehanna Township School District
Harrisburg, Pennsylvania

Pamela Bauer
Speech/Language Pathologist, M.A., CCC/SLP
Special School District of St. Louis County
Kindergarten Interventionist
Arrowpoint Elementary
Hazelwood, Missouri

James Brohn
Principal
Morning Star Lutheran School
Jackson, Wisconsin

Earl S. Brown
Teacher: Middle School Math
Susquehanna Township Middle School
Susquehanna Township School District
Harrisburg, Pennsylvania

Rebecca Centerino
Teacher: Grade 1
Zitzman Elementary
Meramec Valley RIII School District
Pacific, Missouri

Jessica Z. Jacobs
Assistant Principal
Thomas Holtzman Junior Elementary School
Susquehanna Township School District
Harrisburg, Pennsylvania

Tonya Leonard
Teacher: Grade 3
Peine Ridge Elementary
Wentzville RIV School District
Wentzville, Missouri

Jennifer Love Frier
Teacher: Grade 1
Olathe School District
Olathe, Kansas

Michelle Mieger
Teacher: Grade 3
Cedar Springs Elementary
Northwest R-1
House Springs, Missouri

Jeanne K. Selissen
Teacher: Grade 4
Tewksbury School District
Tewksbury, Massachusetts

Jo Ellen Showers
Teacher: Grade K
Sara Lindemuth Primary School
Susquehanna Township School District
Harrisburg, Pennsylvania

Judith M. Stagoski
Grades Taught: 5–8
District: Archdiocese of St. Louis
St. Louis, Missouri

Pauline Von Hoffer
Grades Taught: 4–12
Curriculum Coordinator
Wentzville School District
Wentzville, Missouri

© Houghton Mifflin Harcourt Publishing Company • Image Credits: (bg) ©Peter Dazeley/Photographer's Choice RF/Getty Images

Go Math! and the Principles of Effective Mathematics Programs

All education researchers strongly agree that two components of effective mathematics programs have a positive impact on student learning: the implemented curriculum and teachers' implementation of research-informed instructional practices.

PROFESSIONAL DEVELOPMENT **by Matthew R. Larson, Ph.D.**
K-12 Curriculum Specialist for Mathematics
Lincoln Public Schools
Lincoln, Nebraska

Go Math! uniquely provides both elements: a strong curriculum aligned to current expectations, and a design that robustly supports teachers' research-informed instructional practices.

The Curriculum

The power of the curriculum to affect how much students learn in mathematics is well established (Marzano, 2003; Schmoker, 2011). The National Council of Teachers of Mathematics (2014, p. 70) has argued that "an excellent mathematics program includes curriculum that develops important mathematics along coherent learning progressions."

That is precisely how we designed *Go Math!* Its scope and sequence are designed in accord with the latest research on learning progressions (Clements and Sarama, 2014). The curriculum makes connections between and among various mathematical topics, and it is coherent, rigorous, and focused.

The favorable outcome is that students learn each grade level's important mathematics at a deep level while simultaneously connecting each lesson to the bigger ideas of mathematics. In *Go Math!* an optimal proportion of the tasks students work on to develop their understanding as well as their proficiency require complex thought and reasoning – the tasks are not merely harder.

Research-Informed Instructional Practices

A coherent and rigorous curriculum is one of two critical components of a mathematics program that helps ensure the success of all students. The second critical component is an instructional approach based on research-informed instructional practices. The overarching message in NCTM's publication *Principles to Actions: Ensuring Mathematical Success for All* is that "effective teaching is the nonnegotiable core that ensures all students learn mathematics at high levels" (NCTM, 2014, p. 4). NCTM offers eight research-informed instructional strategies to support effective teaching and learning of mathematics. *Go Math!* embeds those eight instructional strategies in the curriculum. These strategies are shown in the table on page PG19.

Embedded Professional Development Support

As authors we appreciate that you are being asked to teach more mathematics at deeper levels than ever before. Teaching mathematics effectively is a complex endeavor, and it takes time to integrate new instructional strategies into your practice. Toward that end *Go Math!* embeds professional development resources into the curriculum. In a series of professional development videos, *Go Math!* coauthor Juli Dixon models successful teaching practices and strategies in real classrooms. These videos are an invaluable resource as you work collaboratively with your colleagues to ensure that all students successfully attain the standards and that you grow in your own knowledge of mathematics and highly effective instructional strategies.

Instructional Strategies...	**In *Go Math!*...**
1 Establish mathematics goals to focus learning. Effective teaching establishes clear goals, situates goals within learning progressions, and uses the goals to guide instructional decisions (NCTM, 2014, p. 12).	*The goals are clearly labeled in Go Math! More importantly, the scope and sequence have been built around learning progressions and the big ideas of mathematics.*
2 Implement tasks that promote reasoning and problem solving. Effective teaching engages students in solving and discussing tasks that promote mathematical reasoning and problem solving and allow multiple entry points and varied solution strategies (NCTM, 2014, p. 17).	*The 5E lesson framework in Go Math! helps ensure that students explore worthwhile mathematical tasks in every lesson to develop their understanding.*
3 Use and connect mathematical representations. Effective teaching engages students in making connections to deepen understanding of concepts and procedures and as tools for problem solving (NCTM, 2014, p. 24).	*Students move systematically from concrete representations, to their own drawn representations on their MathBoards, and finally to symbolic mathematics.*
4 Facilitate meaningful mathematical discourse. Effective teaching facilitates discourse among students to build shared understanding by analyzing and comparing student approaches and arguments (NCTM, 2014, p. 29).	*Math Talk is a central feature of Go Math! Question prompts and sample dialogue in the Teacher Edition support you as you engage students to develop their conceptual understanding.*
5 Pose purposeful questions. Effective teaching uses purposeful questions to assess and advance students' reasoning and sense making (NCTM, 2014, p. 35).	*The Teacher Edition has many question prompts you can use to generate mathematical discourse, determine what students currently know, and advance their learning. These prompts allow you to transform your classroom into an interactive, student-centered learning environment.*
6 Build procedural fluency from conceptual understanding. Effective teaching builds fluency with procedures so that students become skillful in using procedures flexibly as they solve contextual and mathematical problems (NCTM, 2014, p. 42).	*The goal in Go Math! is for students to learn efficient methods for solving procedures based on understanding. Student learning of traditional algorithms starts with concrete models connected to underlying concepts. Eventually students draw their own representations and finally work with efficient algorithms so their proficiency prepares them to learn future mathematics.*
7 Support productive struggle in learning mathematics. Effective teaching consistently provides students with opportunities and supports to engage in productive struggle as they grapple with mathematical ideas and relationships (NCTM, 2014, p. 48).	*The 5E lesson framework supports students' continued engagement with mathematical concepts. Students have ample time to explore concepts prior to the explain phase of the lesson and are supported with significant guided practice as part of the elaborate phase.*
8 Elicit and use evidence of student thinking. Effective teaching uses evidence of student thinking to assess progress and to adjust instruction continually in ways that support and extend learning (NCTM, 2014, p. 53).	*The question prompts as well as Show What You Know in each chapter, Share and Show with Quick Check in each lesson, Mid-Chapter Checkpoints, and Summative Assessment options at the end of each chapter provide teachers continual and real-time options to use evidence of student thinking to adjust and guide instruction. These diagnostic assessments provide teachers differentiated instructional materials to support all students.*

Math Processes and Practices

PROFESSIONAL DEVELOPMENT

by Juli K. Dixon, Ph.D.
Professor, Mathematics Education
University of Central Florida
Orlando, Florida

Developing Processes and Proficiencies in Mathematics Learners

According to *Principles to Actions* (National Council of Teachers of Mathematics, 2014), "An excellent mathematics program requires effective teaching that engages students in meaningful learning through individual and collaborative experiences that promote their ability to make sense of mathematical ideas and reason mathematically" (p. 5). What this means for elementary school students and how to engage students in this sort of meaningful learning is addressed in the following article.

There are eight Mathematical Processes and Practices. They are based on the National Council of Teachers of Mathematics' (NCTM) *Process Standards* (NCTM, 2000) and the National Research Council's (NRC) *Strands of Mathematical Proficiency* (NRC, 2001). Students who are engaged in the mathematical processes and practices around important mathematics are likely engaged in meaningful learning as described in *Principles to Actions*.

It is likely that good teachers can find evidence of each of these standards for mathematical practice in their current teaching. Regardless, it is useful to examine them and think about how each contributes to the development of mathematically proficient students. What follows is a description of how they might look in an elementary school classroom. Each of these examples is reflective of experiences supported by *Go Math!*

Go Math! supports the Math Processes and Practices through several specific features including:

- Lessons focused on depth of content knowledge,

- Unlock the Problem sections to begin lessons,

- Math Talk questions prompting students to use varied strategies and to explain their reasoning,

- Support for manipulative use and drawings directly on the student pages,

- Prompts that lead students to write their own problems or to determine if the reasoning of others is reasonable, and

- Real-world problems that encourage students to develop productive dispositions.

MPPI: Problem Solving

This process brings to mind developing a productive disposition as described in *Adding It Up* (NRC, 2001). In order for students to develop the diligence intended with this process, they must be provided with problems for which a pathway toward a solution is not immediately evident. If students are asked to determine how much of a cookie each person would receive if 4 cookies were shared among 5 people, a solution pathway is evident if students understand fractions. The students could simply divide each cookie into five equal pieces and give each person one fifth of each cookie or $\frac{4}{5}$ of a cookie in all. Now, consider the same problem given the constraint that the first three cookies are each broken into two equal pieces to start and each person is given half of a cookie.

The problem is now more interesting and challenging. How will the remaining pieces of cookies be distributed among the five people? How will the students determine how much of a cookie each person has in all when all the cookies are shared? The students will likely refer back to the context of the problem to make sense of how to solve it. They will also very likely use pictures in their solution process. A solution is within reach, but it will require diligence to persevere in reaching it.

MPP2: Abstract and Quantitative Reasoning

Story problems provide important opportunities for young learners to make sense of mathematics around them. Students often use strategies including acting out the problem to make sense of a solution path. Another important strategy is for students to make sense of the problem situation by determining a number sentence that could represent the problem and then solving it in a mathematically proficient way. Consider the following problem: *Jessica has 7 key chains in her collection. How many more does she need to have 15 key chains all together?*

A student is presented with this problem, but rather than focusing on key words, the student uses the story to make sense of a solution process. The student knows to start with 7 then add something to that to get 15. The student represents this story abstractly by writing $7 + \underline{} = 15$. Then the student reasons quantitatively by thinking $7 + 3 = 10$ and $10 + 5 = 15$, so $7 + 8$ must equal 15 (because 3 and 5 are 8). The student then returns to the problem to see if a solution of 8 key chains makes sense. In doing so, the student makes "sense of quantities and their relationships in problem situations" (NGA Center/CCSSO, 2010, p. 6).

MPP3: Use and Evaluate Logical Reasoning

Students need to explain and justify their solution strategies. They should also listen to the explanations of other students and try to make sense of them. They will then be able to incorporate the reasoning of others into their own strategies and improve upon their own solutions. An example of this follows.

A group of students explores formulas for areas of quadrilaterals. Students make sense of the formula for the area of a parallelogram as $b \times h$ by decomposing parallelograms and composing a rectangle with the same area. Following this exploration, a student conjectures that the formula for the area of the trapezoid is also $b \times h$. The student draws this picture and says that the trapezoid can be "turned into" a rectangle with the same base by "moving one triangle over to the other side."

This student has constructed a viable argument based on a special type of trapezoid. Another student agrees that this formula works for an isosceles trapezoid but asks if it will also work for a general trapezoid. This second student has made sense of the reasoning of the first student and asked a question to help improve the argument.

MPP4: Mathematical Modeling

Students need opportunities to use mathematics to solve real-world problems. As students learn more mathematics, the ways they model situations with mathematics should become more efficient. Consider the problem: *Riley has 4 blue erasers, Alex has 4 yellow erasers, and Paige has 4 purple erasers. How many erasers do they have in all?* A young student would likely model this problem with $4 + 4 + 4$. However, a mathematically proficient student in third grade should model the same situation with 3×4. This demonstrates how modeling will evolve through a student's experiences in mathematics and will change as his or her understanding grows.

A useful strategy for making sense of mathematics is for students to develop real-life contexts to correspond to mathematical expressions. This supports the reflexive relationship that if a student can write a word problem for a given expression, then the student can model a similar word problem with mathematics. Consider $\frac{4}{5} - \frac{1}{2}$. If a student is able to create a word problem to support this fraction subtraction, then, given a word problem, the student is more likely to be able to model the word problem with mathematics and solve it.

MPP5: Use Mathematical Tools

At first glance, one might think that this practice refers to technological tools exclusively, however, tools also include paper and pencil, number lines, and manipulatives (or concrete models). Mathematically proficient students are able to determine which tool to use for a given task. An example to illustrate this practice involves multiplying fractions. A student might choose to use a number line for one problem and paper and pencil procedures for another. If presented the problem $\frac{1}{3} \times \frac{3}{4}$, a mathematically proficient student might draw a number line and divide the distance from 0 to 1 into 4 equal parts drawing a darker line through the first three fourths. That student would see that $\frac{1}{3}$ of the $\frac{3}{4}$ is $\frac{1}{4}$ of the whole.

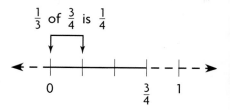

However, the same student presented with the problem $\frac{1}{3} \times \frac{4}{7}$ might not use a drawing at all, but might find it more efficient to multiply the numerators and the denominators of the factors to get $\frac{4}{21}$ as the product. Both solution paths illustrate strategic use of tools for the given problems.

MPP6: Use Precise Mathematical Language

An important aspect of precision in mathematics is developed through the language used to describe it. This can be illustrated with definitions of geometric shapes. A kindergarten student is not expected to classify quadrilaterals. However, it is appropriate for a kindergarten student to name and describe shapes including squares and rectangles. Teachers seeking to support kindergarten students to attend to precision will include squares within sets of other rectangles so that these students will not use the language that all rectangles have two long sides and two short sides. These same students will be more likely to be able to correctly classify squares and rectangles in third grade because of this attention to precision when they are in kindergarten.

MPP7: See Structure

Students who have made sense of strategies based on properties for finding products of single digit factors (basic facts) will be more likely to apply those properties when exploring multidigit multiplication. Consider the importance of the distributive property in looking for and making use of structure in this case. A student who has made sense of 6×7 by solving 6×5 and 6×2 has used a strategy based on the distributive property where 6×7 can be thought of as $6 \times (5 + 2)$ and then the 6 can be "distributed over" the 5 and 2. This same student can apply the distributive property to make sense of 12×24 by thinking of 24 as $20 + 4$ and solving $12 \times 20 + 12 \times 4$. A student who can make sense of multidigit multiplication in this way is on a good path to making sense of the structure of the standard algorithm for multidigit multiplication.

MPP8: Generalize

Whether performing simple calculations or solving complex problems, students should take advantage of the regularity of mathematics. If students who are exploring the volume of right rectangular prisms are given centimeter cubes and grid paper, they can build a prism with a given base and explore how the volume changes as the height of the prism increases. Students who look for ways to describe the change should see that the height of the prism is a factor of the volume of the prism and that if the area of the base is known, the volume of the prism is determined by multiplying the area of the base by the height of the prism. Identifying this pattern and repeated reasoning will help students build an understanding of the formula for the volume of right rectangular prisms.

As evidenced by the examples of mathematical processes and practices in elementary school classrooms, "a lack of understanding effectively prevents a student from engaging in the mathematical practices" (NGA Center/CCSSO, 2010, p. 8). Teachers address this challenge by focusing on mathematical processes and practices while developing an understanding of the content they support. In so doing, this process facilitates the development of mathematically proficient students.

Supporting Math Processes and Practices Through Questioning

When you ask...	Students...
• What is the problem asking? • How will you use that information? • What other information do you need? • Why did you choose that operation? • What is another way to solve that problem? • What did you do first? Why? • What can you do if you don't know how to solve a problem? • Have you solved a problem similar to this one? • When did you realize your first method would not work for this problem? • How do you know your answer makes sense?	Use problem solving.
• What is a situation that could be represented by this equation? • What operation did you use to represent the situation? • Why does that operation represent the situation? • What properties did you use to find the answer? • How do you know your answer is reasonable?	Use abstract and quantitative reasoning.
• Will that method always work? • How do you know? • What do you think about what she said? • Who can tell us about a different method? • What do you think will happen if...? • When would that not be true? • Why do you agree/disagree with what he said? • What do you want to ask her about that method? • How does that drawing support your work?	Use and evaluate logical reasoning.
• Why is that a good model for this problem? • How can you use a simpler problem to help you find the answer? • What conclusions can you make from your model? • How would you change your model if...?	Use mathematical modeling.
• What could you use to help you solve the problem? • What strategy could you use to make that calculation easier? • How would estimation help you solve that problem? • Why did you decide to use...?	Use mathematical tools.
• How do you know your answer is reasonable? • How can you use math vocabulary in your explanation? • How do you know those answers are equivalent? • What does that mean?	Use precise mathematical language.
• How did you discover that pattern? • What other patterns can you find? • What rule did you use to make this group? • Why can you use that property in this problem? • How is that like...?	See structure.
• What do you remember about...? • What happens when...? • What if you...instead of...? • What might be a shortcut for...?	Generalize.

Math Processes and Practices in *Go Math!*

Math Processes and Practices	Throughout *Go Math!* Look for...	Explanation
1. Problem Solving Mathematically proficient students start by explaining to themselves the meaning of a problem and looking for entry points to its solution. They analyze givens, constraints, relationships, and goals. They make conjectures about the form and meaning of the solution and plan a solution pathway, rather than simply jumping into a solution attempt. They consider analogous problems and try special cases and simpler forms of the original problem in order to gain insight into its solution. They monitor and evaluate their progress and change course if necessary. Mathematically proficient students check their answers to problems using a different method, and they continually ask themselves, "Does this make sense?" and "Is my answer reasonable?" They understand the approaches of others to solving complex problems and identify correspondences between different approaches. Mathematically proficient students understand how mathematical ideas interconnect and build on one another to produce a coherent whole.	**Some Examples:** **Problem Solving Lessons** Grade K, Lesson 1.9 Grade 1, Lesson 8.8 Grade 2, Lesson 1.7 **Unlock the Problem** Grade K, Lesson 2.4 Grade 1, Lesson 3.12 Grade 2, Lesson 6.6	**Children learn to:** • analyze a problem. • explain what information they need to find to solve the problem. • determine what information they need to use to solve the problem. • develop a plan for solving the problem. • use concrete objects to conceptualize a problem. • draw quick pictures on MathBoards to help solve problems. • evaluate the solution for reasonableness.
	Try Another Problem Grade K, Lesson 7.6 Grade 1, Lesson 6.8 Grade 2, Lesson 1.7 **Share and Show** Grade 1, Lesson 7.3 Grade 2, Lesson 10.2 **On Your Own** Grade K, Lesson 4.5 Grade 1, Lesson 10.6 Grade 2, Lesson 5.8	**Children learn to:** • look at similar problems and apply techniques used in the original problem to gain insight into the solution of a new problem. • draw quick pictures on MathBoards to help solve problems. • evaluate the solution for reasonableness. • persevere in solving a problem, determining what methods and strategies they have learned that they can apply to solve the problem.

Teacher Edition   Student Edition

Math Processes and Practices	Throughout *Go Math!* Look for...	Explanation
2. Abstract and Quantitative Reasoning Mathematically proficient students make sense of quantities and their relationships in problem situations. They bring two complementary abilities to bear on problems involving quantitative relationships: the ability to decontextualize—to abstract a given situation and represent it symbolically and manipulate the representing symbols as if they have a life of their own, without necessarily attending to their referents—and the ability to contextualize, to pause as needed during the manipulation process in order to probe into the referents for the symbols involved. Quantitative reasoning entails habits of creating a coherent representation of the problem at hand; considering the units involved; attending to the meaning of quantities, not just how to compute them; and knowing and flexibly using different properties of operations and objects.	**Some Examples:** Model and Draw Grade K, Lesson 5.6 Grade 1, Lesson 3.7 Grade 2, Lesson 3.7	**Children learn to:** • abstract a real-world situation and represent it symbolically as a number sentence as a way of solving a problem. • put the numbers and symbols in a number sentence back into the context of the real-world situation for the solution.
	Measurement and Geometry Lessons Grade K, Lesson 12.5 Grade 1, Lesson 11.2 Grade 2, Lesson 8.1	**Children learn to:** • focus on the meaning of quantities in measurement and geometry problems. • choose the most appropriate kind of unit to use to solve a problem.
	Lessons on the properties of operations Grade K, Lesson 6.3 Grade 1, Lesson 3.7 Grade 2, Lesson 3.1	**Children learn to use these properties of operations:** • changing the way addends are grouped in an addition problem does not change the sum. • changing the order of the addends in an addition problem does not change the sum.
	Lessons on modeling with manipulatives and drawings Grade K, Lesson 5.1 Grade 1, Lesson 5.6 Grade 2, Lesson 3.9	**Children learn to:** • represent real-world situations with concrete and pictorial models. • use bar models as one way to visualize addition and subtraction problems symbolically.

Teacher Edition   Student Edition

Math Processes and Practices	Throughout *Go Math!* Look for...	Explanation
3. Use and Evaluate Logical Reasoning Mathematically proficient students understand and use stated assumptions, definitions, and previously established results in constructing arguments. They make conjectures and build a logical progression of statements to explore the truth of their conjectures. They analyze situations by breaking them into cases and recognize and use counterexamples. They organize their mathematical thinking, justify their conclusions and communicate them to others, and respond to the arguments of others. They reason inductively about data, making plausible arguments that take into account the context from which the data arose. Mathematically proficient students are also able to compare the effectiveness of two plausible arguments, distinguish correct logic or reasoning from that which is flawed, and—if there is a flaw in an argument—explain what it is. They justify whether a given statement is true always, sometimes, or never. Mathematically proficient students participate and collaborate in a mathematics community. They listen to or read the arguments of others, decide whether they make sense, and ask useful questions to clarify or improve the arguments.	**Some Examples:** Math Talk Grade 1, Lesson 8.1 Grade 2, Lesson 11.1	**Children learn to:** • use mathematical language. • explain mathematical concepts. • defend, justify, or disprove a mathematical conjecture. • use deductive reasoning, definitions, and previously proven conclusions.
	Vocabulary Builder Grade K Grade 1 Grade 2 Developing Math Language Grade K Grade 1 Grade 2 Vocabulary Preview Grade 1 Grade 2	**Children learn to:** • develop, build, and reinforce mathematics vocabulary. • discuss mathematical definitions. • strengthen their abilities to communicate ideas about mathematics.
	Think Smarter Problems Grade K, Lesson 5.5 Grade 1, Lesson 9.1 Grade 2, Lesson 1.3 Go Deeper Grade K, Lesson 5.5 Grade 1, Lesson 10.4 Grade 2, Lesson 4.3	**Children learn to:** • extend their thinking. • discuss their explanations. • give concrete examples to justify their explanations. • explain and describe mathematical understanding.

Teacher Edition   Student Edition

Math Processes and Practices	Throughout *Go Math!* Look for...	Explanation
4. Mathematical Modeling Mathematically proficient students apply the mathematics they know to solve problems arising in everyday life, society, and the workplace using a variety of appropriate strategies. They create and use a variety of representations to solve problems and to organize and communicate mathematical ideas. Mathematically proficient students apply what they know and are comfortable making assumptions and approximations to simplify a complicated situation, realizing that these may need revision later. They are able to identify important quantities in a practical situation and map their relationships using such tools as diagrams, two-way tables, graphs, flowcharts and formulas. They analyze those relationships mathematically to draw conclusions. They routinely interpret their mathematical results in the context of the situation and reflect on whether the results make sense, possibly improving the model if it has not served its purpose.	**Some Examples:** **Unlock the Problem • Real World** Grade K, Lesson 6.3 Grade 1, Lesson 7.4 Grade 2, Lesson 8.5	**Children learn to:** • apply the mathematics they know to solve real-world problems. • write a number sentence to describe a situation. • use diagrams, tables, and graphs to help them see relationships and draw conclusions in problems.
	Hands On Lessons Grade K, Lesson 6.4 Grade 1, Lesson 2.8 Grade 2, Lesson 7.4	**Children learn to:** • model in a 'hands-on' approach to analyze problems.
	Connect To... Cross-Curricular Grade K Grade 1 Grade 2 **Literature** Grade K Grade 1 Grade 2	**Children learn to:** • apply the mathematics they know to solve problems in Literature, Science, Social Studies, Art, and other disciplines. • appreciate how mathematics influences their lives in ways both large and small.

Teacher Edition   Student Edition

Math Processes and Practices	Throughout *Go Math!* Look for...	Explanation
5. Use Mathematical Tools Mathematically proficient students consider the available tools when solving a mathematical problem. These tools might include pencil and paper, models, a ruler, a protractor, a calculator, a spreadsheet, a computer algebra system, a statistical package, or dynamic geometry software. Mathematically proficient students are sufficiently familiar with tools appropriate for their grade or course to make sound decisions about when each of these tools might be helpful, recognizing both the insight to be gained and their limitations. Mathematically proficient students identify relevant external mathematical resources, such as digital content, and use them to pose or solve problems. They use technological tools to explore and deepen their understanding of concepts and to support the development of learning mathematics. They use technology to contribute to concept development, simulation, representation, reasoning, communication and problem solving.	**Some Examples:** Hands-On Lessons Grade K, Lesson 3.1 Grade 1, Lesson 12.3 Grade 2, Lesson 8.1	**Children learn to:** • use available tools to analyze problems through a concrete 'hands-on' approach.
	Geometry and Measurement Lessons Grade K, Lesson 11.4 Grade 1, Lesson 9.4 Grade 2, Lesson 8.8	**Children learn to use appropriate tools to:** • enhance and deepen their understanding of measurement and geometry concepts.
	Digital Path *i*Tools **Animated Math Models** **HMH Mega Math** All student lessons	**Children learn to use technological tools to:** • enhance and deepen their understanding of concepts. • enable them to visualize problems. • explore consequences of varying the data given.
6. Use Precise Mathematical Language Mathematically proficient students communicate precisely to others. They use clear definitions, including correct mathematical language, in discussion with others and in their own reasoning. They state the meaning of the symbols they choose, including using the equal sign consistently and appropriately. They express solutions clearly and logically by using the appropriate mathematical terms and notation. They specify units of measure and label axes to clarify the correspondence with quantities in a problem. They calculate accurately and efficiently and check the validity of their results in the context of the problem. They express numerical answers with a degree of precision appropriate for the problem context.	Math Talk Grade 1, Lesson 12.1 Grade 2, Lesson 5.4	**Children learn to:** • communicate precisely. • use mathematical vocabulary to communicate their ideas and explanations and to justify their thinking and solutions.
	Skill Lessons on number sentences and comparisons Grade K, Lesson 5.7 Grade 1, Lesson 7.4 Grade 2, Lesson 2.12	**Children learn to:** • state the meaning of the symbols $(+, -, <, >, =)$ they use in mathematical expressions and sentences accurately. • use the equal sign appropriately. • calculate accurately. • use comparison symbols $(<, >)$ appropriately.
	Measurement Lessons Grade 2, Lesson 8.6	**Children learn to:** • use correct measurement units for solutions.

Teacher Edition   Student Edition

Math Processes and Practices	Throughout *Go Math!* Look for...	Explanation
7. See Structure Mathematically proficient students look closely to discern a pattern or structure. They step back for an overview and shift perspective. They recognize and use properties of operations and equality. They organize and classify geometric shapes based on their attributes. They see expressions, equations, and geometric figures as single objects or as being composed of several objects.	**Some Examples:** Lessons with patterns Grade K, Lesson 9.11 Grade 1, Lesson 6.1 Grade 2, Lesson 1.8	**Children learn to:** • sort shapes according to attributes. • use mathematical vocabulary to communicate their ideas and explanations and to justify their thinking and solutions. • use familiar patterns in our number system to extend counting sequences.
	Geometry Lessons Grade 1, Lesson 11.4 Grade 2, Lesson 11.3	**Children learn to:** • verify that a new three-dimensional shape can be composed by combining three-dimensional shapes. • recognize and identify shapes by the number of side and vertices. • apply the structure of the base-ten number system to deeper understanding of the values of multi-digit numbers.
	Lessons with basic facts Grade 1, Lesson 3.6 Grade 2, Lesson 3.7	**Children learn to:** • use a variety of different strategies to find the sums and differences of basic facts. • use benchmark number 10 when finding differences.
8. Generalize Mathematically proficient students notice if calculations are repeated and look for general methods and shortcuts. They notice regularity in mathematical problems and their work to create a rule or formula. Mathematically proficient students maintain oversight of the process, while attending to the details as they solve a problem. They continually evaluate the reasonableness of their intermediate results.	Lessons with basic facts Grade K, Lesson 6.7 Grade 1, Lesson 5.2 Grade 2, Lesson 3.3	**Children learn to:** • find patterns in basic-fact strategies, such as the 'make a ten' 'doubles plus 1' and 'double minus 1'. • see the relationship between addition and subtraction. • recognize how structure and calculations are repeated as they build fact families. • discover shortcuts for finding sums of basic facts and for recognizing counting patterns.
	Multi-digit Computation Lessons Grade 1, Lesson 8.8 Grade 2, Lesson 6.7	**Children learn to:** • repeat the same steps for each place-value position in the standard algorithm for multi-digit computation.
	Lessons on Comparing Numbers Grade K, Lesson 4.7 Grade 1, Lesson 7.3 Grade 2, Lesson 2.12	**Children learn to:** • model and compare numbers to determine which is less or greater.

Teacher Edition   Student Edition

Big Idea

Develop a conceptual understanding of concepts and strategies for addition and subtraction.

Personal Math Trainer

Look for this symbol for a gateway to your personalized learning path!

Operations and Algebraic Thinking

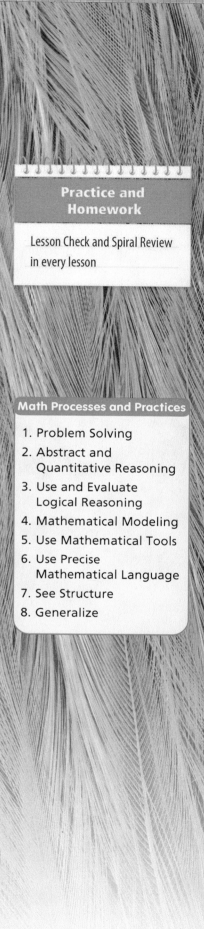

Practice and Homework

Lesson Check and Spiral Review in every lesson

Math Processes and Practices

1. Problem Solving
2. Abstract and Quantitative Reasoning
3. Use and Evaluate Logical Reasoning
4. Mathematical Modeling
5. Use Mathematical Tools
6. Use Precise Mathematical Language
7. See Structure
8. Generalize

© Houghton Mifflin Harcourt Publishing Company • Image Credits: (r) Photodisc/Getty Images

Key: SE—Student Edition; **TE**—Teacher Edition

Number and Operations in Base Ten

Big Idea

Develop a conceptual understanding of place value.

Practice and Homework

Lesson Check and Spiral Review in every lesson

Math Processes and Practices

1. Problem Solving
2. Abstract and Quantitative Reasoning
3. Use and Evaluate Logical Reasoning
4. Mathematical Modeling
5. Use Mathematical Tools
6. Use Precise Mathematical Language
7. See Structure
8. Generalize

Key: SE—Student Edition; **TE**—Teacher Edition

© Houghton Mifflin Harcourt Publishing Company • Image Credits: (r) Photodisc/Getty Images

Measurement and Data

Big Idea

Measure using non-standard units and develop a conceptual understanding of time. Represent data in picture graphs, bar graphs, and tally charts.

Practice and Homework

Lesson Check and Spiral Review in every lesson

Math Processes and Practices

1. Problem Solving
2. Abstract and Quantitative Reasoning
3. Use and Evaluate Logical Reasoning
4. Mathematical Modeling
5. Use Mathematical Tools
6. Use Precise Mathematical Language
7. See Structure
8. Generalize

Key: SE—Student Edition; **TE**—Teacher Edition

© Houghton Mifflin Harcourt Publishing Company • Image Credits: (r) ©Corbis

Big Idea

Identify, describe, and combine both two- and three-dimensional shapes. Develop a conceptual understanding of equal and unequal parts.

Personal Math Trainer

Look for this symbol for a gateway to your personalized learning path!

Geometry

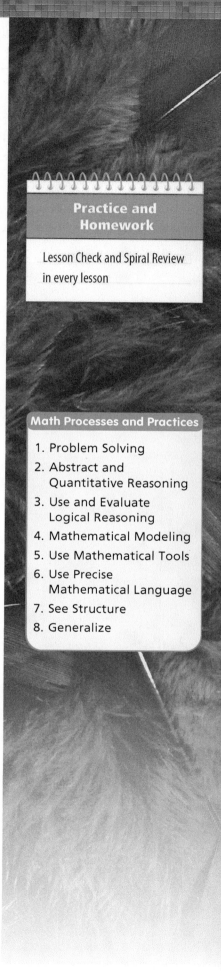

Practice and Homework

Lesson Check and Spiral Review in every lesson

Math Processes and Practices

1. Problem Solving
2. Abstract and Quantitative Reasoning
3. Use and Evaluate Logical Reasoning
4. Mathematical Modeling
5. Use Mathematical Tools
6. Use Precise Mathematical Language
7. See Structure
8. Generalize

© Houghton Mifflin Harcourt Publishing Company • Image Credits: (r) ©Artville/Getty Images

Key: SE—Student Edition; **TE**—Teacher Edition

End-of-Year Resources

Projects

Getting Ready for Grade 2

Key: P—Online Projects; **PG**—Planning Guide

© Houghton Mifflin Harcourt Publishing Company • Image Credits: (l) Photodisc/Getty Images

Teacher Notes

Online Projects

Review Project:
Make a Math Facts Strategies Book

BIG IDEA Develop a conceptual understanding of concepts and strategies for addition and subtraction.

Resources
- Planning Guide, p. PG42

Review Project:
Numbers Around Us

BIG IDEA Develop a conceptual understanding of place value.

Resources
- Planning Guide, p. PG44

Review Project:
Measure and Graph

BIG IDEA Measure using non-standard units and develop a conceptual understanding of time. Represent data in picture graphs, bar graphs, and tally charts.

Resources
- Planning Guide, p. PG46

Review Project:
Building Shapes

BIG IDEA Identify, describe, and combine both two- and three-dimensional shapes. Develop a conceptual understanding of equal and unequal parts.

Resources
- Planning Guide, p. PG48

- Animated Math Models
- Assessment
- HMH Mega Math
- iTools
- Projects
- Multimedia *e*Glossary

Getting Ready Lessons build on Grade 1 content and prepare students for Grade 2 content.

Daily Pacing Chart

Review Projects	Lessons	Assessment	Total
4 days	20 days	2 days	26 days

LESSON 1   ALGEBRA • **Ways to Expand Numbers**

Resources
- Student Lesson Pages, Online
- Planning Guide, p. PG50

LESSON 5   ALGEBRA • **Subtraction Function Tables**

Resources
- Student Lesson Pages, Online
- Planning Guide, p. PG58

LESSON 6   ALGEBRA • **Follow the Rule**

Resources
- Student Lesson Pages, Online
- Planning Guide, p. PG60

 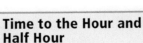

LESSON 10   **Repeated Addition**

Resources
- Student Lesson Pages, Online
- Planning Guide, p. PG68

LESSON 11   **Use Repeated Addition to Solve Problems**

Resources
- Student Lesson Pages, Online
- Planning Guide, p. PG70

LESSON 15   **Time to the Hour and Half Hour** ✓

Resources
- Student Lesson Pages, Online
- Planning Guide, p. PG80

LESSON 16   **Use a Picture Graph**

Resources
- Student Lesson Pages, Online
- Planning Guide, p. PG82

LESSON 20   **Equal Shares** ✓

Resources
- Student Lesson Pages, Online
- Planning Guide, p. PG90

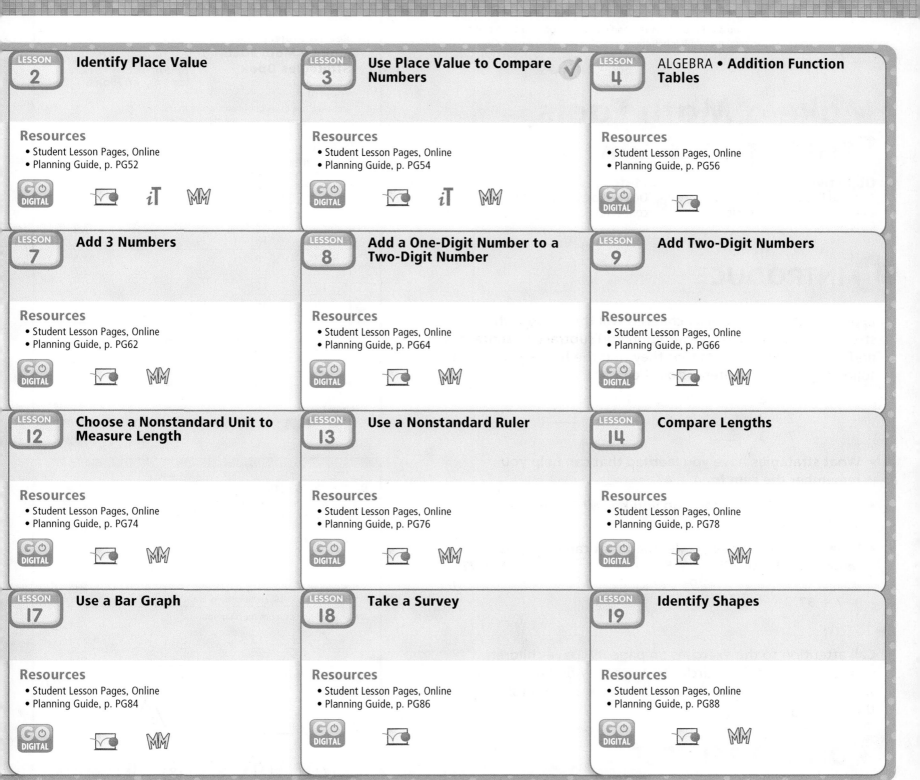

LESSON 2 Identify Place Value

Resources
- Student Lesson Pages, Online
- Planning Guide, p. PG52

LESSON 3 Use Place Value to Compare Numbers ✓

Resources
- Student Lesson Pages, Online
- Planning Guide, p. PG54

LESSON 4 ALGEBRA • Addition Function Tables

Resources
- Student Lesson Pages, Online
- Planning Guide, p. PG56

LESSON 7 Add 3 Numbers

Resources
- Student Lesson Pages, Online
- Planning Guide, p. PG62

LESSON 8 Add a One-Digit Number to a Two-Digit Number

Resources
- Student Lesson Pages, Online
- Planning Guide, p. PG64

LESSON 9 Add Two-Digit Numbers

Resources
- Student Lesson Pages, Online
- Planning Guide, p. PG66

LESSON 12 Choose a Nonstandard Unit to Measure Length

Resources
- Student Lesson Pages, Online
- Planning Guide, p. PG74

LESSON 13 Use a Nonstandard Ruler

Resources
- Student Lesson Pages, Online
- Planning Guide, p. PG76

LESSON 14 Compare Lengths

Resources
- Student Lesson Pages, Online
- Planning Guide, p. PG78

LESSON 17 Use a Bar Graph

Resources
- Student Lesson Pages, Online
- Planning Guide, p. PG84

LESSON 18 Take a Survey

Resources
- Student Lesson Pages, Online
- Planning Guide, p. PG86

LESSON 19 Identify Shapes

Resources
- Student Lesson Pages, Online
- Planning Guide, p. PG88

✓ Assessment

An Assessment Check Mark following a lesson title indicates that a Checkpoint or Getting Ready Test is available for assessment after completing the lesson.

Checkpoints and Getting Ready Tests can be found in the online Getting Ready Lessons and Resources.

Develop a conceptual understanding of concepts and strategies for addition and subtraction.

Make a Math Facts Strategies Book

Objective
Apply addition and subtraction strategies to complete basic facts practice.

Materials
Online Project pp. B9–B12, connecting cubes

1 INTRODUCE

Explain that for this project children will think about the strategies they use to solve addition and subtraction sentences and then review the facts that they find the hardest. Write the following number sentences on the board.

$$4 + 4 = \underline{\quad} \qquad 4 + 5 = \underline{\quad}$$
$$8 + 7 = \underline{\quad} \qquad 9 + 2 = \underline{\quad}$$
$$7 + 3 = \underline{\quad}$$

- **What strategies have you learned that can help you remember the sum for 4 + 4?** doubles; 4 + 4 = 8

- **What other doubles facts do you know?** Make a list of children's responses.

- **What strategies have you learned that can help you remember the sum for 4 + 5?** doubles plus 1; 4 + 5 = 9 **8 + 7?** doubles minus 1; 8 + 7 = 15 **9 + 2?** make a ten or count on; 9 + 2 = 11 **7 + 3?** make a ten or count on; 7 + 3 = 10

▶ Plan

Call attention to the exercises on page B9. Have children work independently to circle the facts they find difficult to solve. Have children solve the circled facts and then share their strategies.

2 DO THE PROJECT

▶ Put It Together

On page B10, discuss as a class how addition and subtraction are related. Then have children summarize the relationship using pictures, numbers, or words.

Have them apply their understanding to write related facts for two facts that they personally find difficult to remember. Encourage children to use connecting cubes to check that their number sentences are correct.

Name _____

**Review Project
Make a Math Facts
Strategies Book**

See Planning Guide • End-of-Year Resources for Lesson Plans.

Project
Make a class book about strategies that can help you remember your math facts.

▶ **Plan**
Look at the facts. Which facts are hard for you? Circle them.
Then find each sum and difference.
Children's circling will vary.

9 +5 14	8 +6 14	4 +7 11	7 +8 15	5 +6 11
7 +6 13	8 +5 13	8 +8 16	4 +8 12	5 +7 12
14 −5 9	14 −7 7	11 −7 4	15 −8 7	11 −6 5
12 −5 7	13 −6 7	16 −7 9	17 −8 9	15 −6 9

Review Project   **B9**

▶ **Put It Together**
How are addition and subtraction related? Use pictures, numbers, or words.

Check children's work.

Answers will vary for the following questions. Possible answers are given.

Write two facts that are hard for you.

$$8 \; \boxed{+} \; 5 = 13 \qquad 17 \; \boxed{-} \; 9 = 8$$

Write the related facts for each hard fact.

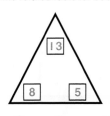

8 + 5 = 13			8 + 9 = 17	
5 + 8 = 13			9 + 8 = 17	
13 − 8 = 5			17 − 9 = 8	
13 − 5 = 8			17 − 8 = 9	

B10

Name _____

Some Fact Strategies
- Doubles
- Doubles plus or minus 1
- Count on or count back
- Make a ten
- Think addition to subtract

▶ **Reflect**

Find each missing number. What strategy did you use? Explain.

Strategies will vary.
Possible answers are given.

1.	$12 - 3 = \underline{9}$	Count back. Think 12. Count back 3 numbers. Say 11, 10, 9. So, $12 - 3 = 9$.
2.	$8 + 9 = \underline{17}$	Use doubles plus 1. Think $8 + 8 = 16$. So, $8 + 8 + 1 = 17$.
3.	$15 - \underline{8} = 7$	Think addition to subtract. 7 plus what number is equal to 15? $7 + 8 = 15$, so $15 - 8 = 7$.
4.	$3 + 9 = \underline{12}$	Count on. Start with 9 because it is the greater number. Count on 3. Think 9. Say 10, 11, 12. So, $9 + 3 = 12$.

Review Project   B11

▶ **Go Beyond**

Write a number from 9 to 14 to use as the whole. Use parts and wholes to complete related number sentences.

Answers will vary. Possible answers are given.

Number: __14__

part	part	whole	whole	part	part
1. 9 + 5 = 14			14 – 5 = 9		
2. 8 + 6 = 14			14 – 6 = 8		
3. 7 + 7 = 14			14 – 7 = 7		
4. 6 + 8 = 14			14 – 8 = 6		
5. 5 + 9 = 14			14 – 9 = 5		

6. Choose one of the number sentences above. What strategy helps you remember how to find the sum or difference?

Answers will vary.

_____

_____

B12

▶ **Reflect**

On page B11, have children explain a strategy that they can use to find each missing number.

▶ **Go Beyond**

On page B12, have children choose a number from 9 to 14 to use as the whole. Then have them use relationships among the parts and the whole to write pairs of related addition and subtraction sentences.

③ EXTEND THE PROJECT

- Have children choose a math fact that they used a strategy to solve. Have them draw a picture to show how the strategy helped them solve the fact.

- Combine children's pages into a class Math Facts Strategies Book.

Performance Assessment You can use this project as a means of assessing a child's understanding of the concepts and skills found in this Big Idea.

Project Scoring Rubric

3 Demonstrates full understanding of the project. Correctly recalls addition and subtraction facts and uses strategies correctly.

2 Demonstrates a thorough understanding of the project. Recalls addition and subtraction facts, that may contain minor errors.

1 Demonstrates a partial understanding of the project. Recalls most of the facts and uses some of the strategies correctly.

0 Demonstrates little understanding of addition and subtraction strategies.

Online Projects, pp. B11–B12

Develop a conceptual understanding of place value.

Numbers Around Us

Objective
Use tens and ones to show whole number relationships.

Materials
Online Project pp. B13–B15, connecting cubes

1 INTRODUCE

Use the question below to introduce the project.

- **How can you use numbers to tell about somebody or something?**

Show children a number that describes you and ask them to guess what it represents. After several guesses, share the answer.

Next, have children write a number that tells something about themselves. Ask for volunteers to share and explain their answers.

▶ Plan

Tell children that they will make a number show by gathering numbers that tell about them and their classmates.

2 DO THE PROJECT

▶ Put It Together

Have children use connecting cubes to show how many pets live in their homes. Ask children to hold up their connected cubes. Children without any pets can assist in collecting and counting the groups of cubes.

- **How can you use connecting cubes to show and count the number of pets there are in our class?** Put our cubes together. Make groups of tens.

- **How many groups of ten? How many ones? How many pets do the children in our class have?**

For Exercise 1 on page B13, have children write the class number of pets and then record the tens and ones by drawing a quick picture. For Exercise 2, have them tell how many children live in their home and show the number with connecting cubes. Have children help count all the cubes by making tens and ones and record by drawing a quick picture.

In Exercise 3 on page B14, have children choose, model, and record their favorite number from 10 to 100. Have children count crayons they have in their desk to complete Exercise 4.

Name _____

Review Project
Numbers Around Us

See Planning Guide • End-of-Year Resources for Lesson Plans.

Project
Make a number show!

▶ **Plan and Put It Together**
Write the number. Show it with a quick picture.

Check children's work.

1. We have ____ pets.

Tens	Ones

____ tens + ____ ones = ____

2. We have ____ children in our class families.

Tens	Ones

____ tens + ____ ones = ____

Review Project   B13

---

3. ____ is my favorite number.   Answers will vary.

Tens	Ones

____ tens + ____ ones = ____

4. I have ____ crayons in my desk.   Answers will vary.

Tens	Ones

____ tens + ____ ones = ____

B14

© Houghton Mifflin Harcourt Publishing Company

Online Projects, pp. B13–B14

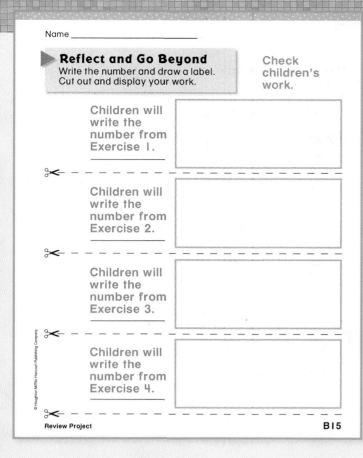

Name _____

▶ **Reflect and Go Beyond**
Write the number and draw a label.
Cut out and display your work.

Check children's work.

Children will write the number from Exercise 1.
_____

✂ - - - - - - - - - - - - - - - - -

Children will write the number from Exercise 2.
_____

✂ - - - - - - - - - - - - - - - - -

Children will write the number from Exercise 3.
_____

✂ - - - - - - - - - - - - - - - - -

Children will write the number from Exercise 4.
_____

✂ - - - - - - - - - - - - - - - - -

Review Project   B15

▶ Reflect

On page B15, have children write each of the four numbers they modeled in Exercises 1–4 on the lines provided. In the box beside each number, have them draw a picture. For example, children may draw a picture of a cat next to the number that tells how many pets the children in the class have.

▶ Go Beyond

Ask children to cut out each number and accompanying picture from the page. Have children glue these numbers and their pictures onto a large piece of paper in numerical order. Children can title this project "Numbers Around Us."

③ EXTEND THE PROJECT

Provide a variety of fun facts that involve numbers from 1 to 100. Here are some examples:

- a female alligator can lay about 60 eggs
- the giant tortoise can live over 100 years
- number of teeth an adult has: 32 teeth
- number of bones in a human hand: 26 bones

Ask children to illustrate their chosen fact on a separate sheet of paper and show the number that describes the fact in words and pictures.

 You can use this project as a means of assessing a child's understanding of the concepts and skills found in this Big Idea.

Project Scoring Rubric
Performance Assessment

3	Demonstrates a full understanding of the project. Is able to represent each number correctly. Is able to order the numbers appropriately.
2	Demonstrates a thorough understanding of the project. Is able to represent most numbers correctly. Is able to order most numbers appropriately.
1	Demonstrates a partial understanding of the project. Is able to represent some numbers correctly. Is able to order some numbers appropriately.
0	Demonstrates little understanding of the project.

Online Projects, p. B15

Measure using non-standard units and develop a conceptual understanding of time. Represent data in picture graphs, bar graphs, and tally charts.

Measure and Graph

Objective
Measure lengths and display the data in a tally chart and a bar graph.

Materials
Online Project pp. B16–B19, classroom objects, paper clip measuring tool, crayons

1 INTRODUCE

Explain that for this project children will measure objects using their paper clip measuring tool, record the lengths, and use a tally chart and a bar graph to display their data.

- **How do you record information in a tally chart?** Possible answer: I draw a tally mark for each object I count. If I count a group of 5, I draw 4 tally marks and a slash across them.

- **How do you record information in a bar graph?** Possible answer: I count the number of objects and color a bar so that it lines up with that number.

▶ Plan

Review with children how to measure the length of an object by lining up the end of their measuring tool with the end of the object. Children count how many paper clips long the object is from one end to the other.

2 DO THE PROJECT

▶ Put It Together

Have children find the classroom objects listed on page B16.

- **How many objects do you need to measure?** 7

Have children measure and record the length of each object using their paper clip measuring tool, making sure to measure each object's length to the nearest paper clip. Next, have children record the lengths in the top chart. Then, in the tally chart, have them draw a tally mark for each length they recorded. Make sure children understand that not every row in the tally chart will have an entry.

- **If the pencil, CD case, and marker are each about 5 paper clips long, how will you show this information in the tally chart?** Possible answer: I will draw 3 tally marks next to the number 5.

Name _____

Review Project
Measure and Graph   See Planning Guide • End-of-Year Resources for Lesson Plans

Project
You can collect and display data.

▶ **Plan**
Find objects like these in your classroom.

| pencil | math book | square pattern block | index card |
| 6-cube train | | CD case | marker |

· Use your paper clip measuring tool.

▶ **Put It Together**
· Measure the lengths of the objects.
· Use the tally chart to record the data.
· Make a bar graph to display the data.
· Use the data to answer questions.

B16

Measure the lengths.

Object	Length
pencil	about 5
6-cube train	about 4
math book	about 10
square pattern block	about 1
CD case	about 5
index card	about 4
marker	about 5

Record in the tally chart.

Length	Number of Objects
1	I
2	
3	
4	II
5	III
6	
7	
8	
9	
10	I

Review Project   B17

Name _____

Make a bar graph.

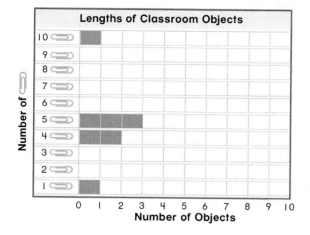

Lengths of Classroom Objects

Number of 🖇

1. What length had the greatest number of objects? __5__ 🖇
2. What lengths had the least number of objects? __1__ 🖇
   __10__ 🖇
3. What is the longest length? __10__ 🖇
4. What is the shortest length? __1__ 🖇

B18

© Houghton Mifflin Harcourt Publishing Company

▶ **Reflect**
How are the tally chart and bar graph alike?
<u>Possible answer: They both show the same</u>
<u>information.</u>

How are they different?
<u>Possible answer: The bar graph shows the</u>
<u>information using bars. A tally chart shows</u>
<u>the information using tally marks.</u>

▶ **Go Beyond**
Find more objects.
Measure them.
Add them to the tally chart and bar graph.
See how the tally chart and bar graph change.

Object	Length

© Houghton Mifflin Harcourt Publishing Company

Review Project   B19

▶ **Reflect**
On page B18, have children use the data from their tally charts to complete the bar graph, then use the bars they colored to answer the questions.

- **How can you use the bar graph to find which length has the greatest number of objects?** Possible answer: After I color the bars for each length, I compare the bars. The longest bar is the length that has the greatest number of objects.

▶ **Go Beyond**
Have classroom objects readily available for children to measure using their paper clip measuring tools. Have them record their measurements on the chart on page B19. Then have children add the new measurements to the tally chart and bar graph. Discuss with children how the tally chart and bar graph change.

③ EXTEND THE PROJECT

- Distribute blank charts to children with the labels "Number of Cubes" and "Length." Have children work in groups to make 10 cube trains of different lengths. Have children record the number of cubes in each train in the chart. Then have children measure each cube train with their paper clip measuring tools and record their measurements in their chart.

- Have groups share their measurements with the class. Then create a bar graph on the board showing the class data.

Portfolio   You can use this project as a means of assessing a child's understanding of the concepts and skills found in this Big Idea.

Project Scoring Rubric

Performance Assessment

3 Demonstrates a full understanding of the project. Accurately measures objects, records data in a tally chart, and completes a bar graph.

2 Demonstrates a thorough understanding of the project. Accurately measures objects, correctly records data in a tally chart, but does not correctly complete a bar graph.

1 Demonstrates a partial understanding of the project. Measures objects and records data in a tally chart with few errors, but does not correctly complete a bar graph.

0 Demonstrates little understanding of measuring, recording data in tally charts, and completing a bar graph.

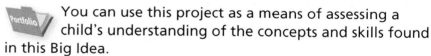

Identify, describe, and combine both two- and three-dimensional shapes. Develop a conceptual understanding of equal and unequal parts.

Building Shapes

Objective
Build two-dimensional and three-dimensional geometric shapes.

Materials
Online Project pp. B20–B23, toothpicks, clay (or mini marshmallows), pattern blocks

1 INTRODUCE

▶ Plan

Introduce the project by reviewing what children know about two-dimensional and three-dimensional shapes.

- **What shapes do you see around the classroom?**

- **How are the shapes the same? How are they different?**

- **Look out the classroom window. What shapes do you see outside?**

Point to different shapes, and have volunteers describe the attributes of each shape. Encourage children to use the number of sides and vertices in their descriptions.

Distribute the project pages and have children preview each page. Then distribute the rest of the materials.

2 DO THE PROJECT

▶ Put It Together

Guide children to use toothpicks and small balls of clay (or mini marshmallows) to make a triangle.

- **How many sides does a triangle have? How many vertices?** three sides; three vertices

- **How can you use the toothpicks and clay (or marshmallows) to build a triangle?** Use toothpicks for the sides and connect them with clay.

Point out that the picture can help them see how to place the toothpicks and the balls of clay.

Have children build a triangle and record the number of sides and vertices in the appropriate space on page B20.

Have children continue in a similar manner on page B21 to make a rectangle, trapezoid, and hexagon and record the attributes. Encourage children to recall that a square is a special kind of rectangle. Remind children that the pictures for each shape can help them build the shapes.

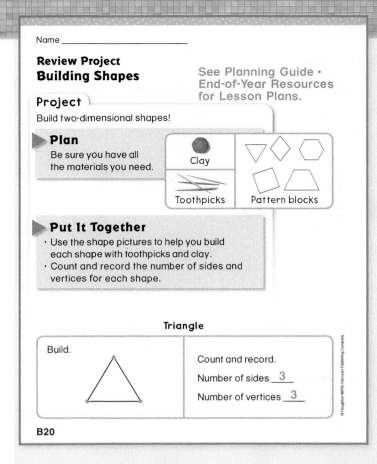

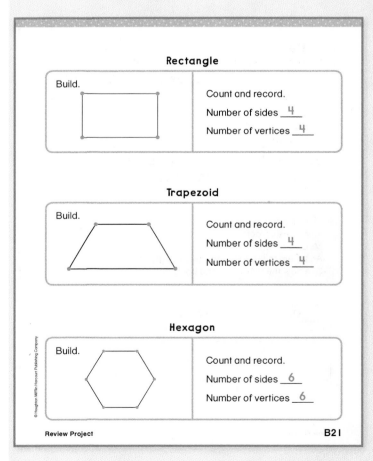

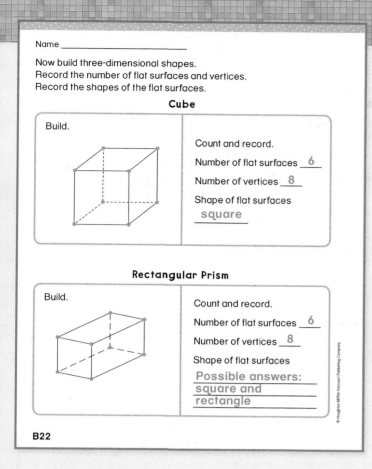

Name _____

Now build three-dimensional shapes.
Record the number of flat surfaces and vertices.
Record the shapes of the flat surfaces.

Cube

Build.

Count and record.

Number of flat surfaces __6__

Number of vertices __8__

Shape of flat surfaces
__square__

Rectangular Prism

Build.

Count and record.

Number of flat surfaces __6__

Number of vertices __8__

Shape of flat surfaces
Possible answers:
__square and__
__rectangle__

B22

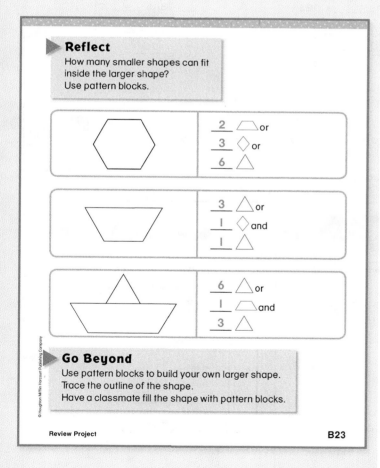

▶ **Reflect**

How many smaller shapes can fit inside the larger shape?
Use pattern blocks.

__2__ ⬠ or
__3__ ◇ or
__6__ △

__3__ △ or
__1__ ◇ and
__1__ △

__6__ △ or
__1__ ⬡ and
__3__ △

▶ **Go Beyond**

Use pattern blocks to build your own larger shape.
Trace the outline of the shape.
Have a classmate fill the shape with pattern blocks.

Review Project   B23

Online Projects, pp. B22–B23

On page B22 discuss the attributes of the shapes, having children record the number of flat surfaces and vertices each shape has as well as the two-dimensional shape(s) of the flat surfaces.

▶ **Reflect**

For page B23, tell children they can use pattern blocks to build the shape with blocks and then trace the blocks.

▶ **Go Beyond**

At the bottom of the page, have children use pattern blocks to build their own shape, trace the outside of the shape, then challenge a classmate to build the shape with pattern blocks.

3 EXTEND THE PROJECT

- Ask children to design a border by laying pattern block trapezoids along a drawn 6-inch line. Have children trace and record the number of shapes used.

- Next, ask children to create the same kind of border using only triangles. Have children record the number of triangles they used. Discuss why they needed more triangles than trapezoids.

Portfolio You can use this project as a means of assessing a child's understanding of the concepts and skills found in this Big Idea.

Project Scoring Rubric

3 Demonstrates a full understanding of the project. Is able to compose and decompose geometric shapes and identify attributes and properties.

2 Demonstrates a thorough understanding of the project. Is able to compose and decompose most geometric shapes and identify most attributes and properties.

1 Demonstrates a partial understanding of the project. Is able to compose and decompose some geometric shapes and identify some attributes and properties.

0 Demonstrates little understanding of the project. Fails to compose and decompose shapes and identify attributes and properties.

LESSON 1

Algebra • Ways to Expand Numbers

LESSON AT A GLANCE

Lesson Objective
Write two-digit numbers in expanded form.

Essential Question
How can you write a two-digit number in different ways?

Materials
MathBoard

GO DIGITAL
- ☑ Animated Math Models
- *i*T *i*Tools: Base-Ten Blocks
- ᗺ HMH Mega Math

1 TEACH and TALK GO DIGITAL • Animated Math Models

▶ **Model and Draw** Math Processes and Practices

Have children count the first set of base-ten models.

- **How many tens are there?** 8 **How many ones?** 7
- **What number does 8 tens stand for?** 80 **What number does 7 ones stand for?** 7
- **What number is 80 plus 7?** 87

2 PRACTICE

▶ **Share and Show** • Guided Practice

- **Look at Exercise 1. Explain how you will write the number in different ways.** First, I will write how many tens (3) and how many ones (5). Then, I will write 3 tens as 30 and 5 ones as 5, or 30 + 5. I will write the number with the 3 as the tens digit and the 5 as the ones digit, or 35.

PG50   Planning Guide

This lesson builds on place value presented in Chapter 6 and prepares children for expanded notation taught in Grade 2.

Name _____

Algebra • Ways to Expand Numbers
Essential Question How can you write a two-digit number in different ways?

See Planning Guide • End-of-Year Resources for Lesson Plans.

Model and Draw

There are different ways to think about a number.

8 tens and 7 ones is the same as 80 plus 7.

$$\underline{8}\ \text{tens}\ \underline{7}\ \text{ones}$$
$$\underline{80} + \underline{7}$$
$$\underline{87}$$

Share and Show MATH BOARD

Write how many tens and ones.
Write the number in two different ways.

1.
$$\underline{3}\ \text{tens}\ \underline{5}\ \text{ones}$$
$$\underline{30} + \underline{5}$$
$$\underline{35}$$

2.
$$\underline{5}\ \text{tens}\ \underline{3}\ \text{ones}$$
$$\underline{50} + \underline{3}$$
$$\underline{53}$$

The 7 represents 70 because the number 72 is made up of 7 tens and 2 ones.

Math Talk   Does the 7 in this number show 7 or 70? Explain.

 72

Getting Ready for Grade 2

one **GR1**

GR: Practice, p. GRP1

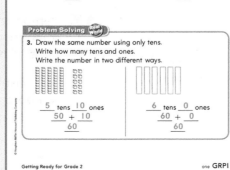

GR: Reteach, p. GRR1

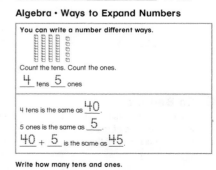

*GR – Getting Ready Lessons and Resources (*www.thinkcentral.com*)

On Your Own

Write how many tens and ones.
Write the number in two different ways.

3.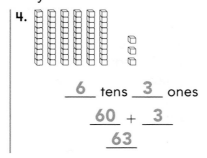

_7_ tens _4_ ones

_70_ + _4_

_74_

4.

_6_ tens _3_ ones

_60_ + _3_

_63_

Problem Solving (Real World)

5. Draw the same number using only tens.
Write how many tens and ones.
Write the number in two different ways.

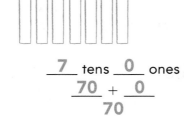

_6_ tens _10_ ones

_60_ + _10_

_70_

_7_ tens _0_ ones

_70_ + _0_

_70_

 TAKE HOME ACTIVITY • Write a two-digit number to 99. Ask your child to write how many tens and ones and then write the number a different way.

GR2 two

© Houghton Mifflin Harcourt Publishing Company

Have children complete Exercise 2.

Use **Math Talk** to ensure that children understand that the 7 in the number 72 represents 7 tens or 70.

▶ **On Your Own**

If children answered Exercises 1–2 correctly, assign Exercises 3–4. It is important that children understand the difference in value between the tens and ones digits.

• **In Exercise 3, what number does the 7 stand for in 74?** 70 **How do you know?** Possible answer: 7 is the digit in the tens place, so it stands for 7 tens. 7 tens is 70.

▶ **Problem Solving**

UNLOCK THE PROBLEM Exercise 5 requires children to use higher order thinking skills. They need to understand that 10 ones is equivalent to 1 ten. It may be helpful to have children use models and match 10 ones next to 1 ten to show they are equivalent. Be sure children understand that they must replace the 10 ones with 1 ten and not just eliminate the ones.

• **Why can you write this number using only tens?** because I can trade the 10 ones for 1 ten

• **What number did you show in two different ways?** 70

3 SUMMARIZE

Math Processes and Practices

Essential Question

How can you write a two-digit number in different ways? I can write a two-digit number by writing the number of tens and the number of ones, like 6 tens 7 ones. Then I can write the number of tens as a number and the number of ones as another number, like 60 + 7. Then I can write the number with 6 as the tens digit and 7 as the ones digit, like 67.

Math Journal  **Math**

Draw quick pictures to show 9 tens 2 ones. Write the number in three different ways.

LESSON **2**

Identify Place Value

LESSON AT A GLANCE

Lesson Objective
Identify how many hundreds, tens, and ones there are in numbers to 199.

Essential Question
How can you use place value to understand the value of a number?

Materials
MathBoard, base-ten blocks

 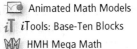

GO DIGITAL

- ☑ Animated Math Models
- *i*T *i*Tools: Base-Ten Blocks
- 〰 HMH Mega Math

1 TEACH and TALK • Animated Math Models

▶ **Model and Draw** Math Processes and Practices

Work through the model with children. Point out that the chart explains what each digit stands for in the number 125.

Focus on the base-ten blocks and the quick pictures. Match them with their digits in the place value chart as you read what each digit in 125 means.

- **What does the place value chart show?**
  how many hundreds, tens, and ones there are in the number 125

2 PRACTICE

▶ **Share and Show** • Guided Practice

- **How will you show each hundred?** I will trace to draw the square.

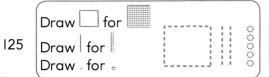

This lesson builds on identifying tens and ones presented in Chapter 6 and prepares children for identifying hundreds, tens, and ones taught in Grade 2.

Name _____

Identify Place Value

Essential Question How can you use place value to understand the value of a number?

Model and Draw

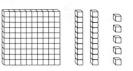

The **1** in 1**25** means 1 hundred.
The **2** in 1**25** means 2 tens.
The **5** in 12**5** means 5 ones.

125
Draw ☐ for ▦
Draw | for |
Draw . for .

hundreds	tens	ones
1	2	5

Share and Show

Use your MathBoard and  to show the number.
Draw to complete the quick picture. Write how many hundreds, tens, and ones.

THINK
106 has no tens.

1.

106

hundreds	tens	ones
1	0	6

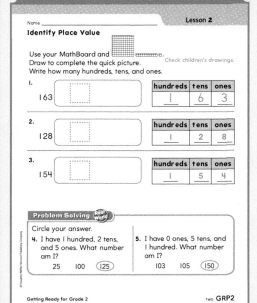 **Math Talk** How is the 1 in 187 different from the 1 in 781?

The 1 in 187 means 1 hundred.
The 1 in 781 means 1 one.

Getting Ready for Grade 2

three **GR3**

GR: Practice, p. GRP2

Name _____ Lesson **2**

Identify Place Value

Use your MathBoard and ▦〰.
Draw to complete the quick picture.
Write how many hundreds, tens, and ones. Check children's drawings.

1.
163

hundreds	tens	ones
1	6	3

2.
128

hundreds	tens	ones
1	2	8

3.
154

hundreds	tens	ones
1	5	4

Problem Solving Real World

Circle your answer.

4. I have 1 hundred, 2 tens, and 5 ones. What number am I?

25   100   (125)

5. I have 0 ones, 5 tens, and 1 hundred. What number am I?

103   105   (150)

Getting Ready for Grade 2

two **GRP2**

GR: Reteach, p. GRR2

Name _____ Lesson 2 Reteach

Identify Place Value

This shows the number 136.

136 has 1 hundred 3 tens 6 ones.

Write the numbers in the table.

hundreds	tens	ones
1	3	6

Draw to show 136.

Draw ☐ for ▦
Draw | for |
Draw . for .

Use your MathBoard and ▦〰.
to show the number. Trace to draw the quick picture.
Write how many hundreds, tens, and ones.

1.
128   Check children's drawings.

hundreds	tens	ones
1	2	8

Reteach
GRR2   Grade 1

---

*GR – Getting Ready Lessons and Resources (*www.thinkcentral.com*)

On Your Own

Use your MathBoard and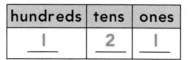
Draw to complete the quick picture.
Write how many hundreds, tens, and ones.

2.

170

hundreds	tens	ones
1	7	0

3.

143

hundreds	tens	ones
1	4	3

4.

121

hundreds	tens	ones
1	2	1

Problem Solving (Real World)

Circle your answer.

5. I have 1 hundred, 9 tens, and 9 ones. What number am I?

99   100   (199)

6. I have 3 ones, 0 tens, and 1 hundred. What number am I?

107   170   (103)

 TAKE HOME ACTIVITY • Write some numbers from 100 to 199. Have your child tell how many hundreds, tens, and ones are in the number.

GR4 four

© Houghton Mifflin Harcourt Publishing Company

- **How will you show tens and ones?** I will draw a line for each ten and a circle for each one.

Have children complete Exercise 1.

Use Math Talk to check that children understand that 1 has a different value in each number because it is in a different place.

▶ On Your Own

If children answered Exercise 1 correctly, assign Exercises 2–4. Point out that when writing a three-digit number with either no tens or no ones, children must write 0 in the correct place.

- **How many hundreds are in the number 170?** 1
- **What does the 7 in the number 170 mean?** There are 7 tens in the number 170.
- **What does the 0 in the number 170 mean?** There are no ones in the number 170.

▶ Problem Solving

UNLOCK THE PROBLEM Exercises 5 and 6 require children to attend to precision. Remind children that the value of a number is determined by the order of the digits.

Go Deeper

- **The numbers 103, 130, and 301 all have the same digits. Why are the numbers different?**
  Each digit has a different value because it is in a different place. The number of hundreds, tens, and ones is different in each number.

(3) SUMMARIZE

Math Processes and Practices

Essential Question

How can you use place value to understand the value of a number? Possible answers: I can tell the value of each digit based on its place in the number. I can tell if the digit means hundreds, tens, or ones.

Math Journal    Math

Tell how many hundreds, tens, and ones are in the number 154.

LESSON 3

Use Place Value to Compare Numbers

LESSON AT A GLANCE

Lesson Objective
Use $<$, $>$, and $=$ to compare numbers.

Essential Question
How can you use place value to compare two numbers?

Materials
MathBoard

 GO DIGITAL

- Animated Math Models
- iTools: Base-Ten Blocks
- HMH Mega Math

1 TEACH and TALK GO DIGITAL • Animated Math Models

▶ **Model and Draw** Math Processes and Practices

Have children tell what it means to compare two numbers.

- **What words can you use to compare two numbers?** I can say which number is greater than, less than, or equal to another number.

Point out that knowing the value of each digit is necessary to compare two numbers.

Compare 134 and 125, focusing on comparing the hundreds first and then the tens.

- **Suppose the hundreds digit and tens digit in two numbers are the same. How can you compare the numbers?** by comparing the ones

---

This lesson builds on comparing two-digit numbers presented in Chapter 7 and prepares children for comparing three-digit numbers taught in Grade 2.

Name _____

Use Place Value to Compare Numbers

Essential Question How can you use place value to compare two numbers?

Model and Draw

I want to eat the greater number.

Use these symbols to compare numbers.

$>$ is greater than
$<$ is less than
$=$ is equal to

45 46

$45 < 46$
45 is less than 46.

Compare 134 and 125.

First compare hundreds.
One hundred is equal to one hundred.
$100 = 100$
If the hundreds are equal, compare the tens. 30 is greater than 20.
$134 > 125$

Share and Show MATH BOARD

Write the numbers and compare. Write $>$, $<$, or $=$.

1. $159 > 155$ 2. $138 < 142$

Compare the numbers using $>$, $<$, or $=$.

3. $187 > 168$ 4. $165 > 159$ 5. $127 < 141$

Math Talk Compare 173 and 177. Did you have to compare all the digits? Why or why not?

Yes. The hundreds and tens are the same so compare the ones. 3 ones is less than 7 ones, so 173 is less than 177.

Getting Ready for Grade 2

five **GR5**

GR: Practice, p. GRP3

Name _____   Lesson 3

Use Place Value to Compare Numbers

Write the numbers. Compare. Write $>$, $<$, or $=$.

1. $172 < 176$ 2. $143 > 128$

Compare the numbers using $>$, $<$, or $=$.

3. $162 = 162$ 4. $154 > 148$ 5. $195 < 199$
6. $133 < 137$ 7. $129 > 126$ 8. $141 = 141$
9. $119 < 125$ 10. $173 = 173$ 11. $187 < 192$
12. $153 = 153$ 13. $191 > 178$ 14. $144 < 153$

Problem Solving Real World

Solve.

15. Josh is thinking of a number between 100 and 199. It has 1 hundred, 4 tens, and 9 ones. Pia is thinking of a number between 100 and 199. It has 1 hundred, 8 tens, and 2 ones. Who is thinking of the greater number?

Draw or write to explain.

Check children's work.

Pia is thinking of a greater number.

Getting Ready for Grade 2   three **GRP3**

GR: Reteach, p. GRR3

Name _____   Lesson 3 Reteach

Use Place Value to Compare Numbers

You can use models and symbols to compare numbers.

$>$ means **is greater than**
$<$ means **is less than**
$=$ means **is equal to**

Use the model to compare 142 and 147.

Step 1 Compare the hundreds. 1 hundred = 1 hundred
Step 2 Compare the tens. 4 tens = 4 tens
Step 3 Compare the ones. 2 ones $<$ 7 ones

So, 142 is less than 147. $142 < 147$

Use ▯ if you need to.
Write the numbers and compare. Write $<$, $>$, or $=$.

1. $168 > 166$

Compare the numbers using $>$, $<$, or $=$.
You may wish to make a model to check.

2. $151 = 151$

Reteach   GRR3   Grade 1

---

*GR – Getting Ready Lessons and Resources (www.thinkcentral.com)

On Your Own

Write the numbers. Compare. Write >, <, or =.

6. 153 $<$ 155

7. 136 $>$ 129

Compare the numbers using >, <, or =.

8. 143 $=$ 143
9. 162 $>$ 157
10. 185 $<$ 188

11. 124 $<$ 129
12. 189 $<$ 195
13. 135 $=$ 135

14. 173 $>$ 164
15. 123 $>$ 117
16. 118 $<$ 131

17. 155 $>$ 145
18. 181 $=$ 181
19. 192 $>$ 179

20. 122 $<$ 129
21. 166 $<$ 177
22. 154 $=$ 154

Problem Solving Real World

23. Antonio is thinking of a number between 100 and 199. It has 1 hundred, 3 tens, and 6 ones. Kim is thinking of a number between 100 and 199. It has 1 hundred, 6 tens, and 3 ones. Who is thinking of a greater number?

Draw or write to explain.

Check children's work.

___Kim___ is thinking of a greater number.

 TAKE HOME ACTIVITY • Choose two numbers between 100 and 199 and have your child explain which number is greater.

GR6 six

© Houghton Mifflin Harcourt Publishing Company

Getting Ready Lessons and Resources, pp. GR7–GR8   ✓ Checkpoint

Name _____

✓ Checkpoint

Concepts and Skills

Write how many tens and ones.
Write the number in two ways.

1.
  __4__ tens and __7__ ones
  __40__ + __7__
  __47__

2.
  __6__ tens and __1__ one
  __60__ + __1__
  __61__

Use your MathBoard and .
Draw to complete the quick picture.
Write how many hundreds, tens, and ones.

3. 154

hundreds	tens	ones
1	5	4

4. 128

hundreds	tens	ones
1	2	8

Getting Ready for Grade 2   seven GR7

Write the numbers and compare. Write >, <, or =.

5. 123 $>$ 111

6. 135 $<$ 145

Compare the numbers using >, <, or =.

7. 175 $=$ 175
8. 163 $<$ 173
9. 189 $>$ 188
10. 142 $<$ 158
11. 157 $=$ 157
12. 185 $>$ 180

13. Which comparison is correct?
  ● 132 > 131
  ○ 131 = 132
  ○ 131 > 132

GR8 eight

---

2 PRACTICE

▶ Share and Show • Guided Practice

- **In Exercise 1, is 159 less than, greater than, or equal to 155?** greater than

Use Math Talk to check that children understand that to compare these numbers they must compare the ones because the hundreds and tens digits are the same.

▶ On Your Own

If children answered Exercises 1–5 correctly, assign Exercises 6–22. It is important that children understand that they must always compare the digits one place at a time.

- **What is always the first step in comparing numbers with hundreds, tens, and ones?** Compare the hundreds.

▶ Problem Solving Real World

UNLOCK THE PROBLEM Exercise 23 requires children to make sense of problems. Children will first need to compare the hundreds.

- **How can you tell how many hundreds each of the numbers will have?** Both numbers are between 100 and 199. The numbers from 100 through 199 have 1 in the hundreds place. So, both numbers have 1 in the hundreds place.
- **What will you compare next?** the tens
- **Who is thinking of the greater number?** Kim **Why?** because 6 tens is greater than 3 tens

3 SUMMARIZE

Math Processes and Practices

Essential Question

How can you use place value to compare two numbers? I can compare the value of each digit, one at a time, starting with the hundreds to see which number is greater than, less than, or equal to the other. If the number of hundreds is the same, I can compare the tens. If the hundreds and tens are the same, I can compare the ones.

Math Journal  WRITE Math

Use the numbers 158 and 185. Compare the numbers using >, <, or =.

Getting Ready for Grade 2 Lesson 3   PG55

Algebra: Addition Function Tables

LESSON AT A GLANCE

Lesson Objective
Complete an addition function table.

Essential Question
How can you follow a rule to complete an addition function table?

Materials
MathBoard

GO DIGITAL

☑ Animated Math Models

1 TEACH and TALK GO DIGITAL · Animated Math Models

▶ **Model and Draw** (Math Processes and Practices)

Focus on the Add 9 function table.

- **What does the rule "Add 9" tell you to do?** Add 9 to each number in the left column.

- **What addition sentences can help you complete the function table?** 7 + 9 = 16; 8 + 9 = 17; 9 + 9 = 18

- **Why do you think this is called an addition function table?** because the rule says add

Discuss how the function table works including how following the rule results in a pattern across each row.

- **What pattern do you see when you complete this table?** Each number in the right column is 9 more than the number in the same row in the left column.

This lesson builds on addition facts presented in Chapter 3 and prepares children for addition skills and strategies taught in Grade 2.

Name _____

Algebra • Addition Function Tables

Essential Question How can you follow a rule to complete an addition function table?

Model and Draw

The rule is Add 9. Add 9 to each number.

Add 9	
7	16
8	17
9	18

Share and Show MATH BOARD

Follow a rule to complete the table.

1.

Add 3	
7	10
8	11
9	12

2.

Add 4	
6	10
7	11
8	12

3.

Add 5	
5	10
7	12
9	14

4.

Add 8	
5	13
7	15
9	17

5.

Add 7	
6	13
8	15
9	16

6.

Add 6	
6	12
8	14
9	15

 Math Talk Look at Exercise 4. How does the rule help you see a pattern?

The rule is Add 8, so in each row the number on the right is 8 more than the number on the left.

Getting Ready for Grade 2   nine **GR9**

GR: Practice, p. GRP4

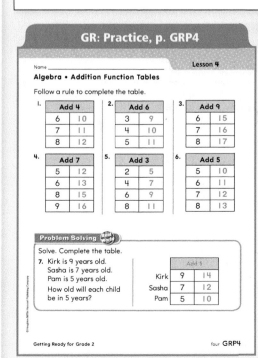

Name _____ Lesson 4

Algebra • Addition Function Tables

Follow a rule to complete the table.

1.

Add 4	
6	10
7	11
8	12

2.

Add 6	
3	9
4	10
5	11

3.

Add 9	
6	15
7	16
8	17

4.

Add 7	
5	12
6	13
8	15
9	16

5.

Add 3	
2	5
4	7
6	9
8	11

6.

Add 5	
5	10
6	11
7	12
8	13

Problem Solving Real World

Solve. Complete the table.

7. Kirk is 9 years old. Sasha is 7 years old. Pam is 5 years old. How old will each child be in 5 years?

Add 5	
Kirk	9	14
Sasha	7	12
Pam	5	10

Getting Ready for Grade 2   four **GRP4**

GR: Reteach, p. GRR4

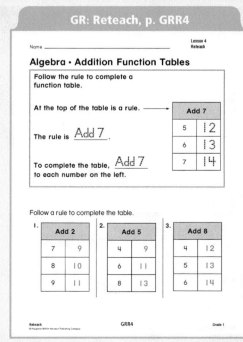

Name _____ Lesson 4 Reteach

Algebra • Addition Function Tables

Follow the rule to complete a function table.

At the top of the table is a rule. ──▶

The rule is Add 7.

To complete the table, Add 7 to each number on the left.

Add 7	
5	12
6	13
7	14

Follow a rule to complete the table.

1.

Add 2	
7	9
8	10
9	11

2.

Add 5	
4	9
6	11
8	13

3.

Add 8	
4	12
5	13
6	14

Reteach   GRR4   Grade 1

*GR – Getting Ready Lessons and Resources (www.thinkcentral.com)

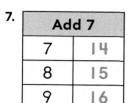

On Your Own

Follow a rule to complete the table.

7.

Add 7	
7	14
8	15
9	16

8.

Add 4	
7	11
8	12
9	13

9.

Add 5	
7	12
8	13
9	14

10.

Add 8	
4	12
6	14
8	16
9	17

11.

Add 3	
3	6
5	8
7	10
9	12

12.

Add 6	
6	12
7	13
8	14
9	15

Problem Solving

13. Solve. Complete the table.

Tom is 8 years old.
Julie is 7 years old.
Carla is 4 years old.

How old will each child
be in 4 years?

	Add 4	
Tom	8	12
Julie	7	11
Carla	4	8

 TAKE HOME ACTIVITY • Copy Exercise 12 and change the numbers in the left column to 9, 7, 5, and 3. Have your child complete the table and explain how he or she used a rule to solve the problem.

GR10 ten

© Houghton Mifflin Harcourt Publishing Company

② PRACTICE

▶ Share and Show • Guided Practice

Check that children are following the rule for each table as they complete Exercises 1–6.

- **How do you know what to do to complete each table?** I read the rule at the top and add that number to each number in left column of the table.

Use Math Talk to help children see that each number in the right column is 8 more than the number in the same row in the left column.

▶ On Your Own

If children answered Exercises 1–6 correctly, assign Exercises 7–12.

- **How are the function tables alike?** They all have addition rules.

- **How are the function tables different?** Each rule has a different number to add.

▶ Problem Solving

UNLOCK THE PROBLEM Exercise 13 requires children to use information from the problem to establish a rule for a function table and to follow the rule to complete the table.

- **What information do you know from reading the problem?** I know how old Tom, Julie, and Carla are.

- **What did you do to solve the problem?** I added 4 to each number. **Explain why.** I wanted to know how old each child will be in 4 years and that means adding 4 to each child's age now.

③ SUMMARIZE

Math Processes and Practices

Essential Question

How can you follow a rule to complete an addition function table? I can add the number shown in the rule to each number in the left column of the table and then write the sum in the right column.

Math Journal   WRITE) Math

What might be the rule for the addition function table if there is a 4 in the left column and an 8 in the right column?

Getting Ready for Grade 2 Lesson 4   PG57

Algebra • Subtraction Function Tables

LESSON AT A GLANCE

Lesson Objective
Complete a subtraction function table.

Essential Question
How can you follow a rule to complete a subtraction function table?

Materials
MathBoard

GO DIGITAL ☑ Animated Math Models

1 TEACH and TALK • Animated Math Models

▶ **Model and Draw** (Math Processes and Practices)

Focus on the Subtract 7 function table.

- **What does the rule "Subtract 7" tell you to do?** Subtract 7 from each number in the left column.
- **What number sentences can help you complete the function table?** $14 - 7 = 7$; $15 - 7 = 8$; $16 - 7 = 9$
- **Why do you think this is called a subtraction function table?** because the rule says subtract

Discuss how the function table works. Guide children to see that the rule makes a pattern across each row.

- **What pattern do you see when you complete this table?** Each number in the right column is 7 less than the number in the same row in the left column.

This lesson builds on subtraction facts presented in Chapter 4 and prepares children for applying subtraction skills and strategies taught in Grade 2.

Name _____

Algebra • Subtraction Function Tables

Essential Question How can you follow a rule to complete a subtraction function table?

Model and Draw

The rule is Subtract 7. Subtract 7 from each number.

Subtract 7	
14	7
15	8
16	9

Share and Show (MATH BOARD)

Follow a rule to complete the table.

1.
Subtract 3	
9	6
10	7
11	8

2.
Subtract 4	
6	2
8	4
10	6

3.
Subtract 5	
6	1
8	3
10	5

4.
Subtract 8	
9	1
11	3
13	5

5.
Subtract 7	
12	5
13	6
14	7

6.
Subtract 6	
6	0
8	2
9	3

Possible answer: I subtract from the same numbers. The differences in Exercise 3 should each be 1 less, because I subtract 5 instead of 4.

Math Talk How can Exercise 2 help you solve Exercise 3?

Getting Ready for Grade 2

eleven **GR11**

© Houghton Mifflin Harcourt Publishing Company

GR: Practice, p. GRP5

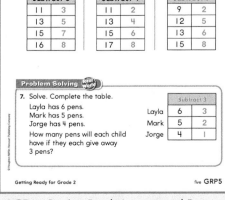

GR: Reteach, p. GRR5

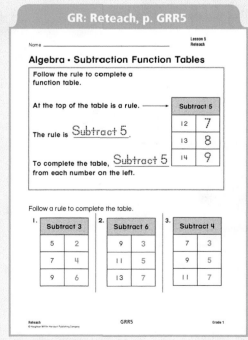

*GR – Getting Ready Lessons and Resources (*www.thinkcentral.com*)

On Your Own

Follow a rule to complete the table.

7.

Subtract 4	
11	7
12	8
13	9

8.

Subtract 6	
7	1
8	2
9	3

9.

Subtract 5	
7	2
8	3
9	4

10.

Subtract 7	
13	6
14	7
15	8
16	9

11.

Subtract 8	
12	4
14	6
16	8
17	9

12.

Subtract 9	
12	3
14	5
16	7
17	8

Problem Solving

13. Solve. Complete the table.

Jane has 4 cookies.
Lucy has 3 cookies.
Seamus has 2 cookies.

How many cookies will each child have if they each eat 2 cookies?

	Subtract 2	
Jane	4	2
Lucy	3	1
Seamus	2	0

 TAKE HOME ACTIVITY • Copy Exercise 12 and change the numbers in the left column to 10, 11, 12, and 13. Have your child complete the table and explain how he or she used a rule to solve the problem.

GR12 twelve

© Houghton Mifflin Harcourt Publishing Company

---

2 PRACTICE

▶ **Share and Show** • **Guided Practice**

Check that children are following the rule for each table as they complete Exercises 1–6.

• **Which numbers would change if you changed the rule for the function table in Exercise 1?** the numbers in the right column

Use Math Talk to focus on similarities and differences in Exercises 2 and 3.

▶ **On Your Own**

If children answered Exercises 1–6 correctly, assign Exercises 7–12.

• **Change the rule in Exercise 12. How does the table change?** Answers will vary.

▶ **Problem Solving**

UNLOCK THE PROBLEM To complete Exercise 13, children have to use information from the problem to establish a rule for a function table and follow the rule to complete the table.

• **What did you do to solve the problem?** I subtracted 2 from each number in the left column. **Explain why.** I wanted to know how many cookies each child will have left if he or she eats 2 cookies and that means subtracting 2 from the number of cookies each child began with.

• **How many cookies will Seamus have if he eats 2 cookies?** 0

3 SUMMARIZE

Math Processes and Practices

Essential Question

How can you follow a rule to complete a subtraction function table? I can subtract the number shown in the rule from each number in the left column of the table and then write how many are left in the right column.

Math Journal WRITE Math

What might be the rule for a subtraction function table if there is a 16 in the left column and a 7 in the right column?

LESSON 6

Algebra • Follow the Rule

LESSON AT A GLANCE

Lesson Objective
Complete addition and subtraction function tables.

Essential Question
How can you follow a rule to complete an addition or subtraction function table?

Materials
MathBoard

 Animated Math Models

1 TEACH and TALK
• Animated Math Models

▶ **Model and Draw** Math Processes and Practices

Compare the function tables at the top of the page.

- **What is the rule for the function table on the left?** add 1 **on the right?** subtract 1
- **How are the two function tables alike?** Both have the same numbers in the left column. **How are they different?** different rules: add 1 and subtract 1

Complete the tables together.

This lesson builds on addition and subtraction facts presented in Chapter 5 and prepares children for patterns and relationships taught in Grade 2.

Name _____

Algebra • Follow the Rule
Essential Question How can you follow a rule to complete an addition or subtraction function table?

Model and Draw

The rule for some tables is to add. For other tables the rule is to subtract.

Add 1	
2	3
4	5
6	7
8	9

Subtract 1	
2	1
4	3
6	5
8	7

Share and Show

Follow a rule to complete the table.

1.
Add 2	
10	12
9	11
8	10
7	9

2.
Subtract 2	
10	8
9	7
8	6
7	5

3.
Subtract 1	
3	2
4	3
7	6
9	8

The rule is Add 2, so in each row the number on the right is 2 more than the number on the left.

 Math Talk What is the rule for the pattern in Exercise 1?

Getting Ready for Grade 2   thirteen **GR13**

GR: Practice, p. GRP6

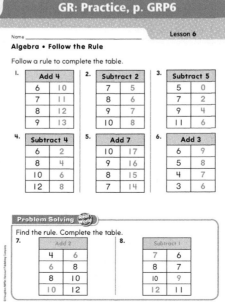

GR: Reteach, p. GRR6

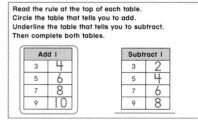

*GR – Getting Ready Lessons and Resources (www.thinkcentral.com)

On Your Own

Follow a rule to complete the table.

4.

Add 5	
7	12
8	13
9	14
10	15

5.

Subtract 5	
7	2
8	3
9	4
10	5

6.

Subtract 1	
8	7
9	8
11	10
13	12

7.

Subtract 3	
5	2
7	4
9	6
11	8

8.

Add 4	
6	10
7	11
8	12
9	13

9.

Add 6	
9	15
8	14
7	13
6	12

Problem Solving Real World

10. Find the rule. Complete the table.

Add 3	
3	6
5	8
7	10
9	12

 TAKE HOME ACTIVITY • Copy the table for Exercise 9.
Change the rule to Subtract 3. Have your child complete the table.

GR14 fourteen

2 PRACTICE

▶ **Share and Show** • Guided Practice

Check that children are following the correct rule.

- **Look at Exercises 1–3. How do you know whether to add or subtract to complete each table?** by looking at the rule at the top of the table

Have children complete Exercises 1–3.

Use Math Talk to have children find patterns by comparing the two columns in a function table and by comparing rows.

▶ **On Your Own**

If children answered Exercises 1–3 correctly, assign Exercises 4–9.

▶ **Problem Solving**

UNLOCK THE PROBLEM Exercise 10 requires children to look for and make use of structure in mathematics. They need to first determine the relationship between the given numbers in a function table in order to establish the rule for the function table. Then children will follow the rule to complete the table.

- **Look at the 7 and 10 in the table. Would you add or subtract to get from 7 to 10?** add **How many would you add?** 3
- **What is the rule for the table?** add 3

Have children complete the table using the rule.

3 SUMMARIZE

Math Processes and Practices

Essential Question

How can you follow a rule to complete an addition or subtraction function table? I can look at the rule that tells how many to add or subtract. I can follow the rule by adding or subtracting the number shown to each number in the left column of the table. I can write my answer in the right column in that row.

Math Journal Math

How do you know if the rule for a function table is to add or subtract?

Getting Ready for Grade 2 Lesson 6   PG61

LESSON 7

Add 3 Numbers

LESSON AT A GLANCE

Lesson Objective
Choose a strategy to add 3 numbers.

Essential Question
How can you choose a strategy to help add 3 numbers?

Materials
MathBoard

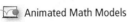

- Animated Math Models
- HMH Mega Math

1 TEACH and TALK ▸ Animated Math Models

▶ **Model and Draw** Math Processes and Practices

Use the example to discuss strategies for adding 3 numbers.

- **How do you use the strategy _make a 10_?** First, I add 2 + 8 to make 10. Then I add on 6.

- **How do you use doubles?** First, I add 8 + 8. Then I add on 4.

- **How do you use the strategy _count on_?** First, I count on 3 from 6 to get 9. Then I add on 8.

- **How do you know which strategy to choose?** I look at the addends to see what is possible. If I have two numbers whose sum is 10, I can make a ten. If I have two of the same number, I can use doubles. If I have 1, 2, or 3 as an addend, I can count on.

Name _____

Add 3 Numbers

Essential Question How can you choose a strategy to help add 3 numbers?

> This lesson builds on addition of 3 numbers presented in Chapter 3 and prepares children for fluent addition within 100 taught in Grade 2.

Model and Draw

When you add 3 numbers, you can add in any order. Using a strategy can help.

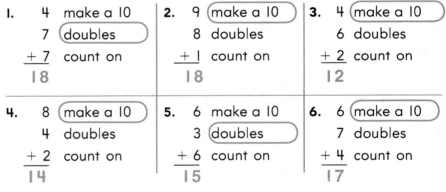

Make a 10.
$$\begin{array}{r} 2 \\ 6 \\ +\,8 \\ \hline 16 \end{array}$$

Use doubles.
$$\begin{array}{r} 8 \\ 8 \\ +\,4 \\ \hline 20 \end{array}$$

Use count on.
$$\begin{array}{r} 6 \\ 8 \\ +\,3 \\ \hline 17 \end{array}$$

Share and Show MATH BOARD

Use strategies to find the sums. Circle any strategy you use.

Possible answers shown.

1. $\begin{array}{r} 4 \\ 7 \\ +\,7 \\ \hline 18 \end{array}$ make a 10 / (doubles) / count on

2. $\begin{array}{r} 9 \\ 8 \\ +\,1 \\ \hline 18 \end{array}$ (make a 10) / doubles / count on

3. $\begin{array}{r} 4 \\ 6 \\ +\,2 \\ \hline 12 \end{array}$ (make a 10) / doubles / count on

4. $\begin{array}{r} 8 \\ 4 \\ +\,2 \\ \hline 14 \end{array}$ (make a 10) / doubles / count on

5. $\begin{array}{r} 6 \\ 3 \\ +\,6 \\ \hline 15 \end{array}$ make a 10 / (doubles) / count on

6. $\begin{array}{r} 6 \\ 7 \\ +\,4 \\ \hline 17 \end{array}$ (make a 10) / doubles / count on

Possible answer: I added 6 + 4 to make a 10. Then I added 10 + 7 to find the sum, 17.

Math Talk Explain why you used the make a 10 strategy to solve Exercise 6.

© Houghton Mifflin Harcourt Publishing Company

Getting Ready for Grade 2

fifteen **GR15**

GR: Practice, p. GRP7

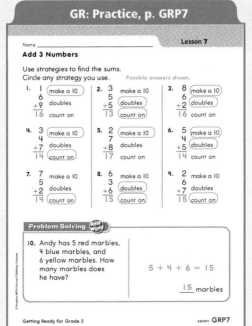

Name _____ Lesson 7

Add 3 Numbers

Use strategies to find the sums.
Circle any strategy you use. Possible answers shown.

1. $\begin{array}{r} 1 \\ 6 \\ +\,9 \\ \hline 16 \end{array}$ (make a 10) / doubles / count on

2. $\begin{array}{r} 3 \\ 5 \\ +\,5 \\ \hline 13 \end{array}$ make a 10 / (doubles) / (count on)

3. $\begin{array}{r} 8 \\ 6 \\ +\,2 \\ \hline 16 \end{array}$ (make a 10) / (doubles) / count on

4. $\begin{array}{r} 3 \\ 4 \\ +\,7 \\ \hline 14 \end{array}$ (make a 10) / doubles / (count on)

5. $\begin{array}{r} 2 \\ 7 \\ +\,8 \\ \hline 17 \end{array}$ (make a 10) / doubles / count on

6. $\begin{array}{r} 5 \\ 4 \\ +\,5 \\ \hline 14 \end{array}$ make a 10 / (doubles) / count on

7. $\begin{array}{r} 7 \\ 5 \\ +\,2 \\ \hline 14 \end{array}$ make a 10 / doubles / (count on)

8. $\begin{array}{r} 6 \\ 3 \\ +\,6 \\ \hline 15 \end{array}$ make a 10 / (doubles) / (count on)

9. $\begin{array}{r} 2 \\ 6 \\ +\,7 \\ \hline 15 \end{array}$ make a 10 / doubles / (count on)

Problem Solving Real World

10. Andy has 5 red marbles, 4 blue marbles, and 6 yellow marbles. How many marbles does he have?

$5 + 4 + 6 = 15$

___15___ marbles

Getting Ready for Grade 2 seven **GRP7**

GR: Reteach, p. GRR7

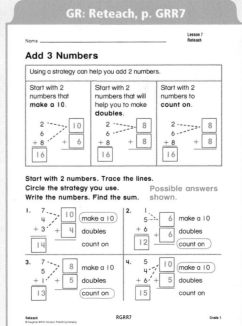

Name _____ Lesson 7 Reteach

Add 3 Numbers

Using a strategy can help you add 2 numbers.

Start with 2 numbers that **make a 10.**	Start with 2 numbers that will help you to make **doubles.**	Start with 2 numbers to **count on.**
$\begin{array}{r} 2 \\ 6 \\ +\,8 \\ \hline 16 \end{array}$ → 10, + 6	$\begin{array}{r} 2 \\ 6 \\ +\,8 \\ \hline 16 \end{array}$ → 8, + 8	$\begin{array}{r} 2 \\ 6 \\ +\,8 \\ \hline 16 \end{array}$ → 8, + 8

Start with 2 numbers. Trace the lines.
Circle the strategy you use.
Write the numbers. Find the sum. Possible answers shown.

1. $\begin{array}{r} 7 \\ 4 \\ +\,3 \\ \hline 14 \end{array}$ → 10, + 4 (make a 10) / doubles / count on

2. $\begin{array}{r} 1 \\ 5 \\ +\,6 \\ \hline 12 \end{array}$ → 6, + 6 make a 10 / (doubles) / (count on)

3. $\begin{array}{r} 7 \\ 5 \\ +\,1 \\ \hline 13 \end{array}$ → 8, + 5 make a 10 / doubles / (count on)

4. $\begin{array}{r} 4 \\ 6 \\ +\,5 \\ \hline 15 \end{array}$ → 10, + 5 (make a 10) / doubles / count on

Reteach RGRR7 Grade 1
© Houghton Mifflin Harcourt Publishing Company

---

*GR – Getting Ready Lessons and Resources (*www.thinkcentral.com*)

On Your Own

Use a strategy to find the sum. Circle the strategy you choose. Possible answers shown.

7.
$$\begin{array}{r} 5 \\ 5 \\ + 5 \\ \hline 15 \end{array}$$
make a 10
(doubles)
count on

8.
$$\begin{array}{r} 7 \\ 3 \\ + 5 \\ \hline 15 \end{array}$$
(make a 10)
doubles
count on

9.
$$\begin{array}{r} 3 \\ 8 \\ + 8 \\ \hline 19 \end{array}$$
make a 10
doubles
(count on)

10.
$$\begin{array}{r} 4 \\ 2 \\ + 7 \\ \hline 13 \end{array}$$
make a 10
doubles
(count on)

11.
$$\begin{array}{r} 2 \\ 9 \\ + 2 \\ \hline 13 \end{array}$$
make a 10
(doubles)
count on

12.
$$\begin{array}{r} 9 \\ 9 \\ + 1 \\ \hline 19 \end{array}$$
make a 10
(doubles)
count on

13.
$$\begin{array}{r} 9 \\ 2 \\ + 8 \\ \hline 19 \end{array}$$
make a 10
doubles
(count on)

14.
$$\begin{array}{r} 6 \\ 3 \\ + 7 \\ \hline 16 \end{array}$$
(make a 10)
doubles
count on

15.
$$\begin{array}{r} 8 \\ 4 \\ + 1 \\ \hline 13 \end{array}$$
make a 10
doubles
(count on)

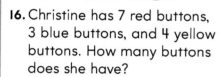

Problem Solving

16. Christine has 7 red buttons, 3 blue buttons, and 4 yellow buttons. How many buttons does she have?

$7 + 3 + 4 = 14$

_14_ buttons

 TAKE HOME ACTIVITY • Ask your child to choose 3 numbers from 1 to 9. Have your child add to find the sum.

© Houghton Mifflin Harcourt Publishing Company

GR16 sixteen

---

2 PRACTICE

▶ **Share and Show** • Guided Practice

• **Look at the addends in Exercise 1. What strategy could you use to find the sum? Why?** I can use doubles because there are two 7s.

Use Math Talk to check children's understanding of using strategies to help them add 3 numbers.

▶ **On Your Own**

If children complete Exercises 1–6 correctly, assign Exercises 7–15. Children should understand they can use any strategy they choose as long as it works for the particular problem.

• **In Exercise 10, can you use doubles to help you add? Why or why not?** No. Possible answer: There are not two addends that are the same number.

▶ **Problem Solving**

UNLOCK THE PROBLEM Children can solve the word problem in Exercise 16 by using a strategy to add the 3 numbers.

• **Did you use a strategy to add? Explain.** Yes. I made a ten by adding 7 + 3. Then I added 10 + 4 to find the sum, 14.

3 SUMMARIZE

Math Processes and Practices

Essential Question

How can you choose a strategy to help add 3 numbers? I look at the addends to see which strategy will work. I might be able to make a ten, use doubles, or count on.

Math Journal WRITE ▶ Math

Use a strategy to add 1 + 8 + 9. Circle the two numbers you added first and tell what strategy you used.

LESSON 8

Add a One-Digit Number to a Two-Digit Number

LESSON AT A GLANCE

Lesson Objective
Find the sum of a 1-digit number and a 2-digit number.

Essential Question
How can you find the sum of a 1-digit number and a 2-digit number?

Materials
MathBoard

✓ Animated Math Models
〽️ HMH Mega Math

---

1 TEACH and TALK · Animated Math Models

▶ **Model and Draw** [Math Processes and Practices]

Have children look at the addends in the sample addition problem.

- **How many tens and ones are in the addends?** 54 is 5 tens and 4 ones. 2 is 2 ones.

- **How many ones are there in all, and how do you know?** There are 6 ones. I add 4 ones and 2 ones.

- **How many tens are there in all?** 5 tens

- **So what is the sum?** 56

PG64   Planning Guide

This lesson builds on addition presented in Chapter 8 and prepares children for fluent addition within 100 taught in Grade 2.

Name _____

Add a One-Digit Number to a Two-Digit Number

Essential Question How can you find the sum of a 1-digit number and a 2-digit number?

Model and Draw

What is 54 + 2?

To find the sum, find how many **tens** and **ones** in all.

	5 tens 4 ones	5 4
	+ 2 ones	+ 2
	5 tens 6 ones	56

Share and Show MATH BOARD

Add. Write the sum.

1. 72	2. 24	3. 41	4. 56
+ 3	+ 1	+ 4	+ 2
75	25	45	58

5. 14	6. 33	7. 61	8. 93
+ 4	+ 6	+ 8	+ 4
18	39	69	97

9. 31	10. 11	11. 40	12. 35
+ 6	+ 7	+ 4	+ 3
37	18	44	38

Possible answer: I added 2 ones from the first addend and 3 ones from the second addend for a total of 5 ones.

 Math Talk How did you find the total number of ones in Exercise 1?

Getting Ready for Grade 2   seventeen **GR17**

GR: Practice, p. GRP8

Name _____   Lesson 8
Add a One-Digit Number to a Two-Digit Number

Add. Write the sum.

1. 34	2. 44	3. 37
+ 5	+ 3	+ 1
39	47	38

4. 37	5. 91	6. 84
+ 1	+ 4	+ 2
38	95	86

7. 45	8. 12	9. 24
+ 3	+ 7	+ 4
48	19	28

10. 32	11. 71	12. 53
+ 5	+ 7	+ 2
37	78	55

Problem Solving (Real World)

13. There are 21 children in the pool. Then 5 more children join them. How many children are in the pool now?

26 children

Getting Ready for Grade 2   eight GRP8

GR: Reteach, p. GRR8

Name _____   Lesson 8
Reteach
Add a One-Digit Number to a Two-Digit Number

Add to find how many **tens** and **ones** in all.
Write the sum.

43
+ 2
45

There are 4 tens. There are 5 ones. The sum is 45.

Add. Write the sum.

1. 32	2. 12
+ 4	+ 7
36	19

3. 53	4. 47
+ 5	+ 2
58	49

5. 68	6. 95
+ 1	+ 3
69	98

Reteach
                 GRR8   Grade 1

---

*GR – Getting Ready Lessons and Resources (*www.thinkcentral.com*)

On Your Own

Add. Write the sum.

13.	22 + 7 29	14.	53 + 3 56	15.	46 + 2 48	16.	71 + 8 79
17.	84 + 5 89	18.	93 + 4 97	19.	16 + 3 19	20.	37 + 1 38
21.	62 + 2 64	22.	23 + 5 28	23.	82 + 2 84	24.	44 + 4 48

Problem Solving

25. There are 23 children in the first grade class. Then 3 more children join the class. How many children are there now?

_26_ children

TAKE HOME ACTIVITY • Tell your child you had 12 pennies and then you got 5 more. Have your child add to find how many pennies in all.

GR18 eighteen

2 PRACTICE

▶ **Share and Show** • Guided Practice

• **Look at Exercise 2. How many tens are there in all? How many ones are there in all?** 2 tens; 5 ones

Use Math Talk to check children's understanding of how to find the total number of ones when adding a 1-digit number to a 2-digit number.

▶ **On Your Own**

If children complete Exercises 1–12 correctly, assign Exercises 13–24. Have children draw a quick picture to show the numbers in Exercise 13.

• **What does your quick picture show?** 22 is 2 tens and 2 ones. 7 is 7 ones. There are 2 tens and 9 ones in all.

▶ **Problem Solving**

UNLOCK THE PROBLEM Read aloud the word problem in Exercise 25.

• **Will you add or subtract to find the number of children? Explain.** I will add because the class has 23 children plus 3 more.

3 SUMMARIZE

Math Processes and Practices

Essential Question

How can you find the sum of a 1-digit number and a 2-digit number? Possible answer: I can find how many tens and ones there are altogether in both addends.

Math Journal  Math

Use words or pictures to tell how to use tens and ones to add 14 + 5.

LESSON 9

Add Two-Digit Numbers

LESSON AT A GLANCE

Lesson Objective
Find the sum of two 2-digit numbers.

Essential Question
How can you find the sum of two 2-digit numbers?

Materials
MathBoard

☑ Animated Math Models
MM HMH Mega Math

1 TEACH and TALK • Animated Math Models

▶ **Model and Draw** `Math Processes and Practices`

Have children look at the sample addition problem.

- **How many tens and ones are in 23?**
  2 tens and 3 ones.

- **How many tens and ones are in 14?**
  1 ten and 4 ones.

Discuss with children the process of adding the tens in each addend and the ones in each addend. Guide children to see that this gives them the sum.

- **How many tens and ones are there in all?**
  3 tens and 7 ones

- **What is the sum?** 37

Name _____

Add Two-Digit Numbers

Essential Question How can you find the sum of two 2-digit numbers?

This lesson builds on addition presented in Chapter 8 and prepares children for fluent addition within 100 taught in Grade 2.

Model and Draw

What is 23 + 14?

You can find how many **tens** and **ones** in all.

2 tens	**3** ones		**2 3**	
+ 1 ten	4 ones		+ 1 4	
3 tens	7 ones		3 7	

Share and Show

Add. Write the sum.

1. 82
    + 12
    94

2. 25
    + 43
    68

3. 15
    + 14
    29

4. 71
    + 12
    83

5. 36
    + 21
    57

6. 43
    + 41
    84

7. 57
    + 32
    89

8. 21
    + 12
    33

9. 12
    + 12
    24

10. 41
    + 21
    62

11. 32
    + 41
    73

12. 51
    + 14
    65

Possible answer: There are 3 tens. I add the tens digits, 2 + 1.

Math Talk How many tens are in 26 + 11? How do you know?

Getting Ready for Grade 2

nineteen **GR19**

GR: Practice, p. GRP9

Name _____   Lesson 9

Add Two-Digit Numbers

Add. Write the sum.

1. 31
    +52
    83

2. 65
    +34
    99

3. 21
    +32
    53

4. 14
    +21
    35

5. 72
    +26
    98

6. 46
    +31
    77

7. 53
    +12
    65

8. 34
    +54
    88

9. 27
    +50
    77

10. 84
    +11
    95

11. 32
    +53
    85

12. 56
    +22
    78

Problem Solving

13. Evan has 15 toy cars. His brother has 13 toy cars. How many toy cars do the boys have together?

    28 toy cars

Getting Ready for Grade 2   nine GRP9

GR: Reteach, p. GRR9

Name _____   Lesson 9 Reteach

Add Two-Digit Numbers

Add to find how many tens and ones in all. Write the sum.

22
+ 13
35

There are 3 tens. There are 5 ones. The sum is 35.

Add. Write the sum.

1. 31
    + 24
    55

2. 65
    + 14
    79

3. 63
    + 25
    88

4. 42
    + 34
    76

5. 81
    + 17
    98

6. 23
    + 33
    56

Reteach   GRR9   Grade 1

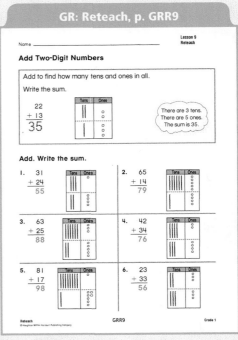

---

*GR – Getting Ready Lessons and Resources (*www.thinkcentral.com*)

On Your Own

Add. Write the sum.

13. 83 + 12 95	14. 73 + 21 94	15. 16 + 51 67	16. 23 + 43 66
17. 24 + 55 79	18. 67 + 21 88	19. 64 + 23 87	20. 51 + 24 75
21. 26 + 32 58	22. 51 + 25 76	23. 46 + 22 68	24. 34 + 45 79

Problem Solving (Real World)

25. Emma has 21 hair clips.
Her sister has 11 hair clips.
How many hair clips do
the girls have together?

_____32_____ hair clips

 TAKE HOME ACTIVITY • Tell your child you drove 21 miles and then you drove 16 more. Have your child add to find how many miles in all.

GR20 twenty

© Houghton Mifflin Harcourt Publishing Company

---

2 PRACTICE

▶ Share and Show • Guided Practice

- **How do you find how many ones in all?**
  I add the ones of both numbers together.
- **How do you find how many tens in all?**
  I add the tens of both numbers together.

Use Math Talk to check children's understanding of adding two 2-digit numbers.

▶ On Your Own

If children completed Exercises 1–12 correctly, assign Exercises 13–24. Some children may benefit by drawing quick pictures to show the problems they find difficult.

- **How can drawing a quick picture help you solve?** A quick picture shows how many tens and ones there are in each addend and how many tens and ones in all.

▶ Problem Solving

UNLOCK THE PROBLEM Discuss the word problem in Exercise 25.

- **What do you know?** Emma has 21 hair clips. Her sister has 11 hair clips.
- **What do you need to find?** how many hair clips in all
- **How will you solve the problem?** I will add 21 + 11.

3 SUMMARIZE

 Math Processes and Practices

Essential Question

How can you find the sum of two 2-digit numbers? I can add the tens of each number together and the ones of each number together to find how many tens and ones there are in all.

Math Journal   WRITE Math

Draw quick pictures to show how to use tens and ones to find 26 + 31.

LESSON 10

Repeated Addition

LESSON AT A GLANCE

Lesson Objective
Use repeated addition to add equal groups.

Essential Question
How can you find how many items there are in equal groups without counting one at a time?

Materials
MathBoard, two-color counters

  Animated Math Models

1 TEACH and TALK  • Animated Math Models

▶ Model and Draw — Math Processes and Practices

Have children use their MathBoards and model the problem with counters.

- **How many groups are there?** 4
- **How many counters are in each group?** 2

Model how to add 2 + 2 + 2 + 2. Say and point to the numbers: **2 + 2 = 4, 4 + 2 = 6, 6 + 2 = 8.**

2 PRACTICE

▶ Share and Show • Guided Practice

Have children complete Exercises 1–3.

Check that children are recording the number in each group on the blanks and not the number of groups.

PG68 Planning Guide

This lesson builds on addition presented in Chapter 5 and prepares children for adding equal groups taught in Grade 2.

Name _____

Repeated Addition

Essential Question How can you find how many items there are in equal groups without counting one at a time?

Model and Draw

When all groups have the same number they are equal groups.

Ayita is putting 2 plants on each step up to her porch. She has 4 steps. How many plants does she need?

There are 4 equal groups. There are 2 in each group. Add to find how many in all.

$\underline{2} + \underline{2} + \underline{2} + \underline{2} = \underline{8}$

Ayita needs $\underline{8}$ plants.

Share and Show

Use your MathBoard and ⬤. Make equal groups. Complete the addition sentence.

	Number of Equal Groups	Number in Each Group	How many in all?
1.	4	3	$\underline{3} + \underline{3} + \underline{3} + \underline{3} = \underline{12}$
2.	2	5	$\underline{5} + \underline{5} = \underline{10}$
3.	3	4	$\underline{4} + \underline{4} + \underline{4} = \underline{12}$

Add: $4 + 4 + 4 + 4 + 4 = 20$

 Math Talk How can you use addition to find 5 groups of 4?

Getting Ready for Grade 2   twenty-one **GR21**

GR: Practice, p. GRP10

Name _____   Lesson 10
Repeated Addition

Use your MathBoard and ⬤. Make equal groups. Complete the addition sentence.

	Number of Equal Groups	Number in Each Group	How many in all?
1.	2	4	$\underline{4} + \underline{4} = \underline{8}$
2.	3	6	$\underline{6} + \underline{6} + \underline{6} = \underline{18}$
3.	4	3	$\underline{3} + \underline{3} + \underline{3} + \underline{3} = \underline{12}$
4.	5	5	$\underline{5} + \underline{5} + \underline{5} + \underline{5} + \underline{5} = \underline{25}$

Problem Solving

Solve.

5. There are 3 bowls. There are 3 apples in each bowl. How many apples are there?

____9____ apples

6. There are 2 shelves. Each shelf has 5 books. How many books are there?

____10____ books

Getting Ready for Grade 2   ten **GRP10**

GR: Reteach, p. GRR10

Name _____   Lesson 10
Reteach
Repeated Addition

Equal groups have the same number of items in each group. You can add equal groups to find how many in all.

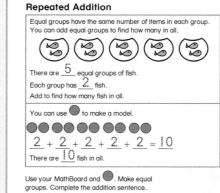

There are $\underline{5}$ equal groups of fish.
Each group has $\underline{2}$ fish.
Add to find how many fish in all.

You can use ⬤ to make a model.

$\underline{2} + \underline{2} + \underline{2} + \underline{2} + \underline{2} = \underline{10}$

There are $\underline{10}$ fish in all.

Use your MathBoard and ⬤. Make equal groups. Complete the addition sentence.

	Number of Equal Groups	Number in Each Group	How many in all?
1.	3	5	$\underline{5} + \underline{5} + \underline{5} = \underline{15}$
2.	4	2	$\underline{2} + \underline{2} + \underline{2} + \underline{2} = \underline{8}$

Reteach   GRR10   Grade 1

---

*GR – Getting Ready Lessons and Resources (*www.thinkcentral.com*)

On Your Own

Use your MathBoard and . Make equal groups. Complete the addition sentence.

	Number of Equal Groups	Number in Each Group	How many in all?
4.	2	3	3 + 3 = 6
5.	3	5	5 + 5 + 5 = 15
6.	4	4	4 + 4 + 4 + 4 = 16
7.	4	5	5 + 5 + 5 + 5 = 20
8.	5	7	7 + 7 + 7 + 7 + 7 = 35

Problem Solving

Solve.

9. There are 3 flower pots. There are 2 flowers in each flower pot. How many flowers are there?

   __6__ flowers

10. There are 2 plants. There are 4 leaves on each plant. How many leaves are there?

   __8__ leaves

TAKE HOME ACTIVITY • Use dry cereal or pasta to make 3 equal groups of 5. Ask your child to find the total number of items.

GR22 twenty-two

- **How did you know what numbers to add in each problem?** I repeated the number that told how many are in each group.

Use Math Talk to make sure children understand that to use repeated addition to find 5 groups of 4, they must add 4 five times.

▶ On Your Own

If children answered Exercises 1–3 correctly, assign Exercises 4–8.

- **How are all the addition sentences you wrote alike?** I add the same numbers two or more times in each addition sentence.

▶ Problem Solving

UNLOCK THE PROBLEM For Exercises 9 and 10, children are asked to complete problems using repeated addition.

- **How can you find the answer to Exercise 9 by adding equal groups?** I can add three groups of 2.
- **How can you find the answer to Exercise 10 by adding equal groups?** I can add two groups of 4.

3 SUMMARIZE

Math Processes and Practices

Essential Question

How can you find how many items there are in equal groups without counting one at a time? I can add the number of items in each group as many times as the number of groups.

Math Journal  Math

Use pictures to show 5 groups that each have 5 marbles. Then write a number sentence to show how to find how many marbles there are in all.

LESSON 11

Use Repeated Addition to Solve Problems

LESSON AT A GLANCE

Lesson Objective
Use repeated addition to solve real world problems.

Essential Question
How can you use repeated addition to solve problems?

Materials
MathBoard, crayons

 GO DIGITAL   **HMH Mega Math**

---

1 TEACH and TALK GO DIGITAL · Animated Math Models

▶ **Model and Draw** Math Processes and Practices

Have children use their MathBoards to record the addition sentence and draw the 3 groups of 4 balloons.

- **How many equal groups are there?** 3
- **How many balloons are in each group?** 4
- **How can you use this information to write a repeated addition sentence?** Possible answer: I can add three 4s, and that is 4 + 4 + 4.
- **How can you solve 4 + 4 + 4?** Possible answer: 4 + 4 = 8, and 8 + 4 = 12. So, Dyanna needs 12 balloons in all.

This lesson builds on addition presented in Chapter 5 and prepares children for repeated addition taught in Grade 2.

Name _____

Use Repeated Addition to Solve Problems

Essential Question How can you use repeated addition to solve problems?

Model and Draw

Dyanna will have 3 friends at her party. She wants to give each friend 4 balloons. How many balloons does Dyanna need?

<u>12</u> balloons

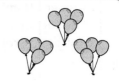

THINK 4 + 4 + 4 = 12

Share and Show MATH BOARD

Draw pictures to show the story.
Write the addition sentence to solve.

1. Ted plays with 2 friends. He wants to give each friend 5 cards. How many cards does Ted need?
   <u>10</u> cards

   Children should draw 2 groups of 5 cards.

   5 + 5 = 10

2. Aisha shops with 4 friends. She wants to buy each friend 2 roses. How many roses does Aisha need?
   <u>8</u> roses

   Children should draw 4 groups of 2 roses.

   2 + 2 + 2 + 2 = 8

   Possible answer: There are 4 friends. Each gets 2 roses, so I used repeated addition and I added 2 + 2 + 2 + 2 = 8.

 Math Talk What pattern can you use to find the answer to Exercise 2?

Getting Ready for Grade 2

twenty-three **GR23**

© Houghton Mifflin Harcourt Publishing Company

GR: Practice, p. GRP11

Name _____   Lesson 11

Use Repeated Addition to Solve Problems

Draw pictures to show the story.
Write the addition to solve.

1. Krista plays with 3 friends. She wants to give each friend 4 pretzels. How many pretzels does Krista need?
   <u>12</u> pretzels

   Children should draw 3 groups of 4 pretzels.

   4 + 4 + 4 = 12

2. Ed plants seeds with 5 friends. He wants to give each friend 5 seeds. How many seeds does Ed need?
   <u>25</u> seeds

   Children should draw 5 groups of 5 seeds.

   5 + 5 + 5 + 5 + 5 = 25

Problem Solving Real World

Circle the way you can model the problem. Then solve.

3. There are 5 friends. Each friend has 4 books. How many books are there?

   5 groups of 5 books
   (5 groups of 4 books)
   4 groups of 5 books

   There are <u>20</u> books.

Getting Ready for Grade 2   eleven **GRP11**

GR: Reteach, p. GRR11

Name _____   Lesson 11 Reteach

Use Repeated Addition to Solve Problems

Loren has 3 jars. She wants to put 5 flowers in each jar. How many flowers does Loren need?

Draw a picture to show the story.

Step 1 Draw <u>3</u> jars.

Step 2 Draw <u>5</u> flowers in each jar.

Step 3 Find how many in all. <u>5</u> + <u>5</u> + <u>5</u> = <u>15</u>

Loren needs <u>15</u> flowers.

Draw pictures to show the story.
Write the addition sentence to solve.

1. Matt plays with 2 friends. He wants to give each friend 4 cars. How many cars does Matt need?
   <u>8</u> cars

   Children should draw 2 groups of 4 cars.

   4 + 4 = 8

2. Liz shops with 3 friends. She wants to buy each friend 3 hair clips. How many hair clips does Liz need?
   <u>9</u> hair clips

   Children should draw 3 groups of 3 hair clips.

   3 + 3 + 3 = 9

Reteach   GRR11   Grade 1
© Houghton Mifflin Harcourt Publishing Company

---

*GR – Getting Ready Lessons and Resources (*www.thinkcentral.com*)

On Your Own

Draw pictures to show the story.
Write the addition sentence to solve.

3. Lea plays with 3 friends. She wants to give each friend 5 ribbons. How many ribbons does Lea need?

__15__ ribbons

Children should draw 3 groups of 5 ribbons.

$$5 + 5 + 5 = 15$$

4. Harry shops with 5 friends. He wants to buy each friend 2 pens. How many pens does Harry need?

__10__ pens

Children should draw 5 groups of 2 pens.

$$2 + 2 + 2 + 2 + 2 = 10$$

5. Cam plays with 4 friends. She wants to give each friend 4 stickers. How many stickers does Cam need?

__16__ stickers

Children should draw 4 groups of 4 stickers.

$$4 + 4 + 4 + 4 = 16$$

Problem Solving Real World

Circle the way you can model the problem. Then solve.

6. There are 4 friends. Each friend has 3 apples. How many apples are there?

4 groups of 4 apples

(4 groups of 3 apples)

3 groups of 4 apples

There are __12__ apples.

 TAKE HOME ACTIVITY • Use small items such as cereal pieces to act out each problem. Have your child check the answers on this page.

GR24 twenty-four

© Houghton Mifflin Harcourt Publishing Company

Getting Ready Lessons and Resources, pp. GR25–GR26   ✓ **Checkpoint**

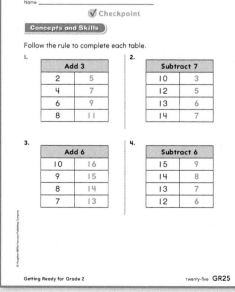

Name _____

✓ Checkpoint

Concepts and Skills

Follow the rule to complete each table.

1.

Add 3	
2	5
4	7
6	9
8	11

2.

Subtract 7	
10	3
12	5
13	6
14	7

3.

Add 6	
10	16
9	15
8	14
7	13

4.

Subtract 6	
15	9
14	8
13	7
12	6

Use strategies to find the sums. Circle any strategy you use.
Possible answers shown.

5.
```
   4      make a 10
   3     (doubles)
 + 4      count on
 ----
  11
```

6.
```
   3     (make a 10)
   7      doubles
 + 5      count on
 ----
  15
```

Add. Write the sum.

7. 32 + 14 = 46

8. 52 + 46 = 98

9. 18 + 21 = 39

10. 43 + 35 = 78

Use your MathBoard and ●. Make equal groups.
Complete the addition sentence.

Number of Equal Groups	Number in Each Group	How many in all?
11. 3	2	2 + 2 + 2 = 6
12. 2	4	4 + 4 = 8

13. Choose the way to model the problem.
James has 4 letters. He puts 2 stamps on each letter.
How many stamps does he use in all?

○ 2 groups of 4 stamps   ○ 4 groups of 4 stamps

○ 2 groups of 2 stamps   ● 4 groups of 2 stamps

Getting Ready for Grade 2   twenty-five **GR25**

GR26 twenty-six

---

2 PRACTICE

▶ **Share and Show** • Guided Practice

Have children complete Exercises 1 and 2. Check that children are drawing pictures and writing a repeated addition sentence to find each answer.

Use **Math Talk** to focus on children's understanding of how they can use a pattern of repeated addition to find the total when adding the same number multiple times.

▶ **On Your Own**

If children answered Exercises 1–2 correctly, assign Exercises 3–5.

• **How many equal groups are there in Exercise 3? How many are in each group?** There are 3 groups. There are 5 in each group.

• **How can drawing a picture help you solve the problem?** Possible answer: I can draw 3 groups of 5 and use the picture to count how many ribbons in all.

▶ **Problem Solving**  Real World

UNLOCK THE PROBLEM For Exercise 6, children are asked to relate their understanding of repeated addition to add equal groups.

• **What addition sentence can help solve this problem? What is the answer?** 3 + 3 + 3 + 3 = 12; There are 12 apples in all.

3 SUMMARIZE

Math Processes and Practices

Essential Question

How can you use repeated addition to solve problems? Possible answer: When a problem has groups with the same number of things, I can add the same number over and over to find the total.

Math Journal WRITE Math

5 friends each have 3 toys. Use numbers and pictures to show the number of toys in all.

Getting Ready for Grade 2
Test
LESSONS 1 TO 11

Summative Assessment

Use the **Getting Ready Test** to assess children's progress in Getting Ready for Grade 2 Lessons 1–11.

Getting Ready Tests are provided in multiple-choice and mixed-response format in the *Getting Ready Lessons and Resources*.

GO DIGITAL Getting Ready Test is available online.

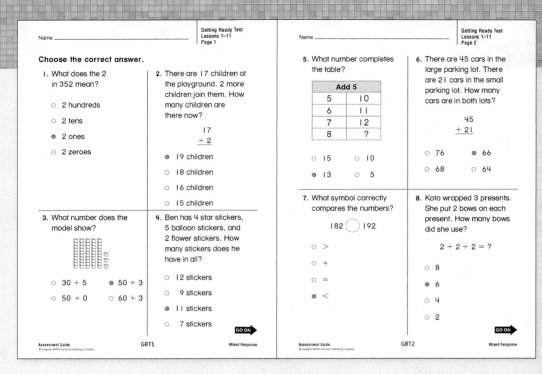

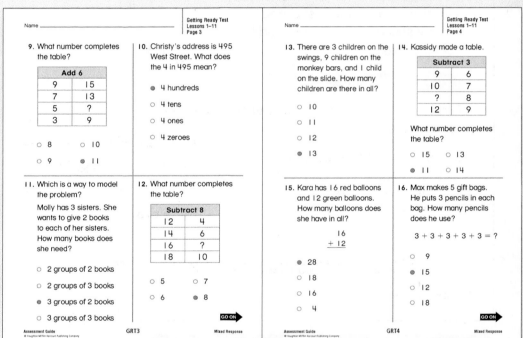

✓ Data-Driven Decision Making ▲ RtI

Item	Lesson	Common Error	Intervene With
1, 10	2	May confuse place value	R—p. GRR2
2, 22	8	May incorrectly add the ones	R—p. GRR8
3, 17, 21	1	May confuse tens and ones	R—p. GRR1
4, 13	7	May not understand how to use strategies to add three numbers	R—p. GRR7
5, 23	4	May not understand which numbers to add	R—p. GRR4
6, 15, 20	9	May incorrectly and ones or tens	R—p. GRR9

Key: R—Getting Ready Lessons and Resources: Reteach

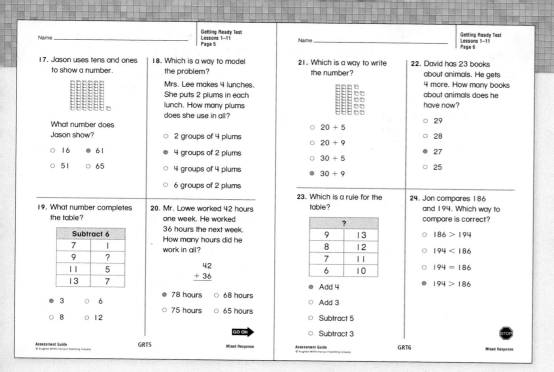

17. Jason uses tens and ones to show a number.

What number does Jason show?

- ○ 16   ● 61
- ○ 51   ○ 65

18. Which is a way to model the problem?

Mrs. Lee makes 4 lunches. She puts 2 plums in each lunch. How many plums does she use in all?

- ○ 2 groups of 4 plums
- ● 4 groups of 2 plums
- ○ 4 groups of 4 plums
- ○ 6 groups of 2 plums

19. What number completes the table?

Subtract 6	
7	1
9	?
11	5
13	7

- ● 3   ○ 6
- ○ 8   ○ 12

20. Mr. Lowe worked 42 hours one week. He worked 36 hours the next week. How many hours did he work in all?

$$\begin{array}{r} 42 \\ + 36 \\ \hline \end{array}$$

- ● 78 hours   ○ 68 hours
- ○ 75 hours   ○ 65 hours

21. Which is a way to write the number?

- ○ 20 + 5
- ○ 20 + 9
- ○ 30 + 5
- ● 30 + 9

22. David has 23 books about animals. He gets 4 more. How many books about animals does he have now?

- ○ 29
- ○ 28
- ● 27
- ○ 25

23. Which is a rule for the table?

?	
9	13
8	12
7	11
6	10

- ● Add 4
- ○ Add 3
- ○ Subtract 5
- ○ Subtract 3

24. Jon compares 186 and 194. Which way to compare is correct?

- ○ 186 > 194
- ○ 194 < 186
- ○ 194 = 186
- ● 194 > 186

Portfolio Suggestions The portfolio represents the growth, talents, achievements, and reflections of the mathematics learner. Children might spend a short time selecting work samples for their portfolios.

You may want to have children respond to the following questions:

- Which question was difficult?
- What would you like to learn more about?

For information about how to organize, share, and evaluate portfolios, see the *Chapter Resources*.

✓ Data-Driven Decision Making ▲ RtI

Item	Lesson	Common Error	Intervene With
7, 24	3	May confuse comparison symbols	R—p. GRR3
8, 16	10	May not understand how to recognize equal groups and find the total number	R—p. GRR10
9, 14	6	May not understand whether to add or subtract, or which numbers to use	R—p. GRR6
11, 18	11	May confuse the number of equal groups and the number in each group	R—p. GRR11
12, 19	5	May subtract incorrectly	R—p. GRR5

Key: R—Getting Ready Lessons and Resources: Reteach

LESSON 12

Choose a Nonstandard Unit to Measure Length

LESSON AT A GLANCE

Lesson Objective
Compare and choose nonstandard units to measure length.

Essential Question
How can you decide which nonstandard unit to use to measure the length of an object?

Materials
MathBoard, paper clips, pencils, connecting cubes, common objects

☑ Animated Math Models

〰 HMH Mega Math

1 TEACH and TALK 〔GO DIGITAL〕 • Animated Math Models

▶ **Model and Draw** 〔Math Processes and Practices〕

Explain that length is the measure of how long an object is.

- **What are some things you would measure with a paper clip?** Possible answers: a stapler, a crayon **What are some things you would measure with a pencil?** Possible answers: a table, a desk

- **Why is it better to use a pencil than a paper clip to measure longer objects? Explain.**
  Possible answer: A pencil is longer than a paper clip. It would take many more paper clips than pencils to measure something long.

This lesson builds on using nonstandard units to measure length presented in Chapter 12 and prepares children for choosing the appropriate unit for measuring length taught in Grade 2.

Name _____

Choose a Nonstandard Unit to Measure Length

Essential Question How can you decide which nonstandard unit to use to measure the length of an object?

〔**Model and Draw**〕

Use ▭ to measure short things.

Use ✏ to measure long things.

〔**Share and Show**〕 〔MATH BOARD〕   Check children's answers.

Use real objects. Circle the unit you would use to measure. Then measure.

	Object	Unit	Measurement
1.	▬	⬭	about ____
2.	✂	⬭	about ____
3.	▯	⬭	about ____
4.	🖍	⬭	about ____

Paper clips; paper clips are shorter than the pencil.

Math Talk Alex measured a book with ▭. Then he measured with ✏. Did he use more ▭ or ✏? Explain.

Getting Ready for Grade 2   twenty-seven **GR27**

© Houghton Mifflin Harcourt Publishing Company

GR: Practice, p. GRP12

Name _____   Lesson 12

Choose a Non-Standard Unit to Measure Length

Use real objects. Choose a unit to   Check children's answers.
measure the length. Then measure.

	Object	Unit	Measurement
1.	✏	⬭ ▪	about ____
2.	ERASER	⬭ ▪	about ____
3.	▭	⬭ ▪	about ____
4.	▱	⬭ ▪	about ____

〔**Problem Solving** Real World〕

5. Shira uses ▪ to measure the fork. Brandon measures the fork and gets a measurement that is less than Shira's measurement. Circle the unit that Brandon uses.

🍴   ⬭   ▪

Getting Ready for Grade 2   twelve GRP12

GR: Reteach, p. GRR12

Name _____   Lesson 12
Reteach

Choose a Non-Standard Unit to Measure Length

You can choose a nonstandard unit to measure the length of real objects.
A ▭ is short. Use it to measure short objects.
A ✏ is longer. Use it to measure long objects.
Circle the unit you would use.
Use ▭ to measure ⌐.
Use ⬭ to measure ▬.

Use real objects. Circle the unit you   Check children's
would use to measure. Then measure.   answers.

	Object	Unit	Measurement
1.	▭	⬭ ✏	about _____
2.	📷	⬭ ✏	about _____
3.	▬	⬭ ✏	about _____

Reteach
© Houghton Mifflin Harcourt Publishing Company   GRR12   Grade 1

---

*GR – Getting Ready Lessons and Resources (www.thinkcentral.com)

On Your Own

Use real objects. Choose a unit to measure the length. Circle it. Then measure.

Ask children to explain their responses.

Object	Unit	Measurement
5. 	🖇 🔲	about ____
6.	🖇 🔲	about ____
7.	🖇 🔲	about ____
8.	🖇 🔲	about ____

Problem Solving (Real World)

9. Fred uses to measure the stick.
Sue measures the stick and gets the same measurement.
Circle the unit that Sue uses.

🖇 🔲

TAKE HOME ACTIVITY • Have your child measure something around the house by using small objects such as paper clips and then by using larger objects such as pencils. Discuss why the measurements differ.

2 PRACTICE

▶ Share and Show • Guided Practice

Model how to use each nonstandard unit to measure the length of a classroom object.

- **Which unit would you use to measure the board?** a pencil **Why?** because a board is long and can be measured with a unit longer than a paper clip

Then have children complete the chart.

Use Math Talk to ensure that children understand that it takes more of a shorter unit than a longer unit to measure the same object.

▶ On Your Own

If children completed Exercises 1–4 correctly, assign Exercises 5–8. You may wish to have children share and compare their answers.

- **Look at Exercise 8. Explain how to use cubes to measure the length of a crayon box.** Possible answer: I would start at one end of the box and place cubes, end to end, along the box. Then I would count the cubes.

▶ Problem Solving (Real World)

UNLOCK THE PROBLEM In order to solve Exercise 9, children need to understand that Sue should use the same unit to get the same measurement.

- **Would Sue and Fred get the same measurement if Sue uses the paper clip? Why or why not?** No; Possible answer: because a paper clip and a cube are not the same length so the measurements will probably not be the same.

3 SUMMARIZE

Math Processes and Practices

Essential Question

How can you decide which nonstandard unit to use to measure the length of an object?

Possible answers: I can choose a unit that is shorter than the object I am measuring. I can choose shorter units to measure shorter objects and longer units to measure longer objects.

Math Journal  Math

Which unit could you use to measure the length of a pencil box? Explain.

Getting Ready for Grade 2 Lesson 12   PG75

LESSON 13

Use a Non-Standard Ruler

LESSON AT A GLANCE

Lesson Objective
Measure length with a nonstandard ruler.

Essential Question
How can you use a nonstandard measuring tool to find length?

Materials
MathBoard

GO DIGITAL

- ▢ Animated Math Models
- ᴍᴍ HMH Mega Math

1 TEACH and TALK 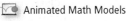 • Animated Math Models

▶ Model and Draw (Math Processes and Practices)

Point out the paper clip ruler at the top of the page.

- **What does the black vertical line at the end of the paper clips show?** that the paper clips and pencil are lined up correctly
- **How do you use the paper clips to find how many paper clips long the pencil is?** I count the paper clips from one end of the pencil to the other.
- **About how long is the pencil?** about 4 paper clips long

2 PRACTICE

▶ Share and Show • Guided Practice

- **Are the paper clips in the correct position in Exercise 1? Explain.** Yes, because the left ends are lined up.

Name _____

Use a Non-Standard Ruler
Essential Question How can you use a non-standard measuring tool to find length?

Model and Draw

About how long is the pencil?

The end of the pencil and the end of the ⚊ must line up. Count how many ⚊ from one end of the pencil to the other.

about __4__ ⚊

Share and Show   MATH BOARD

About how long is the string?

1.

about __2__ ⚊

2.

about __5__ ⚊

Possible answer: If they do not line up, you are measuring more or less than the pencil.

 Math Talk In Exercise 1, why must the end of the pencil and the end of the ⚊ line up?

Getting Ready for Grade 2

twenty-nine **GR29**

© Houghton Mifflin Harcourt Publishing Company

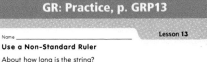

GR: Practice, p. GRP13

Name _____ Lesson 13

Use a Non-Standard Ruler
About how long is the string?

1.

about __9__ ⚊

2.

about __4__ ⚊

3.

about __6__ ⚊

Problem Solving (Real World)

4. Travis measures his marker. He says it is about 7 ⚊ long. Is he correct? Explain.

Possible answer: Yes. The end of the ruler and the end of the marker are lined up. So the measurement is correct.

Getting Ready for Grade 2   thirteen **GRP13**

GR: Reteach, p. GRR13

Name _____ Lesson 13 Reteach

Use a Non-Standard Ruler

Use the ⚊ to measure the marker.

The marker is about __7__ ⚊ long.

How many ⚊ long is the string?

1.

about __8__ ⚊ long

2.

about __5__ ⚊ long

Reteach
© Houghton Mifflin Harcourt Publishing Company   GRR13   Grade 1

***GR** – Getting Ready Lessons and Resources (*www.thinkcentral.com*)

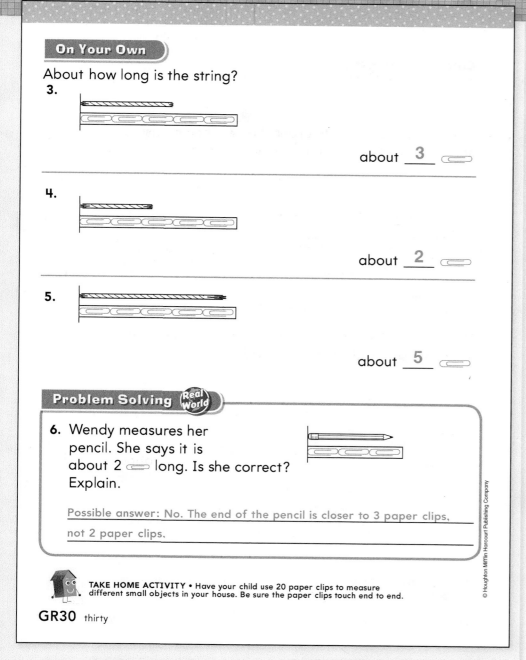

On Your Own

About how long is the string?

3.

about __3__ ⬭

4.

about __2__ ⬭

5.

about __5__ ⬭

Problem Solving Real World

6. Wendy measures her pencil. She says it is about 2 ⬭ long. Is she correct? Explain.

Possible answer: No. The end of the pencil is closer to 3 paper clips, not 2 paper clips.

TAKE HOME ACTIVITY • Have your child use 20 paper clips to measure different small objects in your house. Be sure the paper clips touch end to end.

GR30 thirty

© Houghton Mifflin Harcourt Publishing Company

Use Math Talk to discuss the importance of lining up the object being measured and the measuring tool.

▶ **On Your Own**

If children completed Exercises 1–2 correctly, assign Exercises 3–5.

• **What do you notice about the paper clips?** The paper clips touch each other and do not overlap.

▶ **Problem Solving** Real World

UNLOCK THE PROBLEM Lead a class discussion on accurate measuring techniques. Then have children check to see if Wendy measured correctly in Exercise 6.

• **How do you position a ruler when you measure an object?** I line up the left end of the ruler with the left end of the object.

• **How do you find how many units long the object is?** I count the units from one end of the object to the other.

3 SUMMARIZE

Math Processes and Practices

Essential Question

How can you use a non-standard ruler to measure length? I line up the end of the ruler with the object I am measuring. Then I count the number of units from one end of the object to the other.

Math Journal WRITE Math

Use paper clips. Draw a line that is 6 paper clips long. Label your line.

LESSON 14

Compare Lengths

LESSON AT A GLANCE

Lesson Objective
Compare and then measure lengths with nonstandard units.

Essential Question
How can you compare lengths of objects?

Materials
MathBoard, base-ten unit cubes

GO DIGITAL
- ☑ Animated Math Models
- ⅯⅯ HMH Mega Math

1 TEACH and TALK GO DIGITAL • Animated Math Models

▶ Model and Draw Math Processes and Practices

Materials base-ten unit cubes

Point out the strings at the top of the page.

- **Which string is shortest?** the top string **How can you tell?** The left ends of the strings are lined up. So I look at the right ends to find the shortest string.

- **Use base-ten unit cubes to measure the strings. What lengths are the strings, from shortest to longest?** about 4 cubes, about 6 cubes, about 8 cubes

- **Which string measures the greatest number of cubes?** the longest string

2 PRACTICE MATH BOARD

▶ Share and Show • Guided Practice

- **In Exercise 1, what number do you write to order the shortest string?** 1 **Why does the shortest string come first?** You are ordering from shortest to longest.

Use **Math Talk** to show children that measuring with cubes can be used to determine the order of the strings from shortest to longest.

PG78 Planning Guide

This lesson builds on ordering lengths presented in Chapter 9 and prepares children for comparing standard measurements taught in Grade 2.

Name _____

Compare Lengths

Essential Question How can you compare lengths of objects?

Model and Draw

First, write 1, 2, and 3 to order the strings from **shortest** to **longest**.

Then measure with ▣.

1 ══════════ about __4__ ▣ ←Shortest

3 ══════════════ about __8__ ▣ ←Longest

2 ═════════ about __6__ ▣

Share and Show MATH BOARD

Write 1, 2, and 3 to order the strings from **shortest** to **longest**. Then measure with ▣. Write the lengths.

1. __2__ ══════════ about __5__ ▣

__1__ ═══════ about __3__ ▣

__3__ ═════════════ about __9__ ▣

Possible answer: The string that measures the least number of cubes is shortest. The string that measures the greatest number of cubes is longest.

🦋 **Math Talk** How can measuring with cubes tell you the order of the strings?

Getting Ready for Grade 2

thirty-one **GR31**

© Houghton Mifflin Harcourt Publishing Company

GR: Practice, p. GRP14

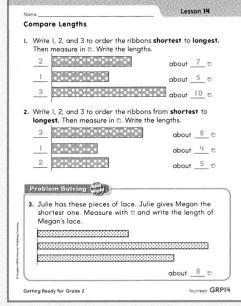

GR: Reteach, p. GRR14

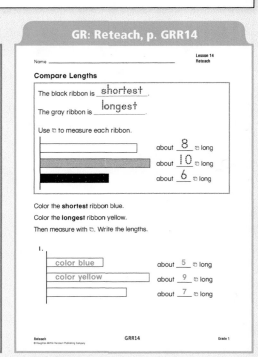

*GR – Getting Ready Lessons and Resources (*www.thinkcentral.com*)

On Your Own

2. Write 1, 2, and 3 to order the strings from **shortest** to **longest**. Then measure with . Write the lengths.

<u> 1 </u>   about <u> 4 </u>

<u> 2 </u>   about <u> 7 </u>

<u> 3 </u>   about <u> 8 </u>

3. Write 1, 2, and 3 to order the strings from **shortest** to **longest**. Then measure with . Write the lengths.

<u> 3 </u>   about <u> 8 </u>

<u> 2 </u>   about <u> 7 </u>

<u> 1 </u>   about <u> 4 </u>

Problem Solving Real World

4. Kate has these ribbons. Kate gives Hannah the longest one. Measure with and write the length of Hannah's ribbon.

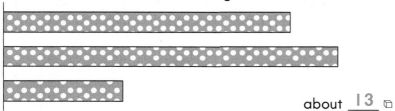

about <u> 13 </u>

TAKE HOME ACTIVITY • Give your child three strips of paper. Have your child cut them about 4 paper clips long, about 2 paper clips long, and about 5 paper clips long. Then have your child order the paper strips from shortest to longest.

GR32   thirty-two

© Houghton Mifflin Harcourt Publishing Company

▶ **On Your Own**

If children complete Exercise 1 correctly, assign Exercises 2 and 3.

• **Predict which string in Exercise 2 will measure the fewest number of cubes.**

Possible answer: the shortest string, the string at the top of the page

▶ **Problem Solving**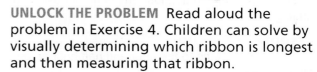

UNLOCK THE PROBLEM Read aloud the problem in Exercise 4. Children can solve by visually determining which ribbon is longest and then measuring that ribbon.

• **Do you need to measure each ribbon? Explain.** No, I only need to measure the longest ribbon because the longest ribbon is Hannah's ribbon.

3 SUMMARIZE

Math Processes and Practices

Essential Question

How can you compare lengths of objects?

I can look at the objects to compare their lengths. Or, I can measure the lengths and compare the measurements.

Math Journal   WRITE Math

Suppose there are three lines, about 2 cubes long, about 4 cubes long, and about 5 cubes long. Are the lines in order from shortest to longest? Write your prediction and then check by drawing the lines.

LESSON 15

Time to the Hour and Half Hour

LESSON AT A GLANCE

Lesson Objective
Tell and write time to the hour and half hour using an analog clock.

Essential Question
How do you tell time to the hour and half hour on an analog clock?

Materials
MathBoard

☑ Animated Math Models
*i*T *i*Tools: Measurement (Clocks)
MM HMH Mega Math

1 TEACH and TALK GO DIGITAL • Animated Math Models

▶ **Model and Draw** Math Processes and Practices

Materials *i*Tools: Measurement (Clocks)

Use the illustrations at the top of the page or the *i*Tools analog clock to review time in hours and half hours. Use clocks that show 4:00 and 4:30.

Direct children's attention to the clock showing 4:00.

- **Where does the hour hand point on this clock?** at 4 **What is the time?** 4:00

Direct children's attention to the clock showing 4:30.

- **Where does the hour hand point on this clock?** halfway between 4 and 5 **What is the time?** 4:30

- **Where does the minute hand point for time to the hour?** at 12 **Where does it point for time to the half hour?** at 6

This lesson builds on time presented in Chapter 9 and prepares children for time taught in Grade 2.

Name _____

Time to the Hour and Half Hour

Essential Question How do you tell time to the hour and half hour on an analog clock?

Model and Draw

The hour hand and the minute hand show the time. Write the time shown on the clock.

4:00   4:30

Share and Show   MATH BOARD

Read the clock. Write the time.

1.   2.   3.

9:30   2:00   3:30

Possible answer: In one hour, the hour hand moves from one number to the next. So, at half past 5:00, the hour hand is halfway between the 5 and 6.

 Math Talk Why does the hour hand point halfway between 5 and 6 at half past 5:00?

Getting Ready for Grade 2   thirty-three **GR33**

© Houghton Mifflin Harcourt Publishing Company

GR: Practice, p. GRP15

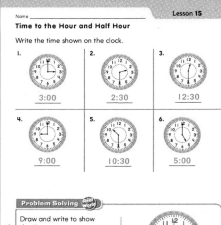

Name _____   Lesson 15

Time to the Hour and Half Hour

Write the time shown on the clock.

1.   2.   3.
3:00   2:30   12:30

4.   5.   6.
9:00   10:30   5:00

Problem Solving
Draw and write to show the time.

7. Kirsten needs to leave for her piano lesson at 4. Draw to show where the hands on the clock will be at that time. Write the time.

4:00

Getting Ready for Grade 2   fifteen **GRP15**

GR: Reteach, p. GRR15

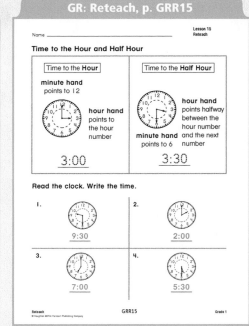

Name _____   Lesson 15 Reteach

Time to the Hour and Half Hour

Time to the **Hour**	Time to the **Half Hour**
minute hand points to 12, hour hand points to the hour number	hour hand points halfway between the hour number and the next number, minute hand points to 6
3:00	3:30

Read the clock. Write the time.

1.   2.
9:30   2:00

3.   4.
7:00   5:30

Reteach   GRR15   Grade 1

---

*GR – Getting Ready Lessons and Resources (*www.thinkcentral.com*)

On Your Own

Read the clock. Write the time.

4.

2:30

5.

12:00

6.

11:30

7.

11:00

8.

6:30

9.

10:00

Problem Solving · Real World

Draw and write to show the time.

10. Liam has soccer practice at half past 10:00.

10:30

 TAKE HOME ACTIVITY · Say a time, such as half past 1:00 or 7:00. Ask your child where the clock hands will point at that time.

GR34 thirty-four

© Houghton Mifflin Harcourt Publishing Company

Getting Ready Lessons and Resources, pp. GR35–GR36 ✓ Checkpoint

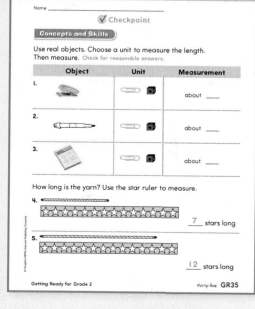

Name _____

✓ Checkpoint

Concepts and Skills

Use real objects. Choose a unit to measure the length. Then measure. Check for reasonable answers.

Object	Unit	Measurement
1.		about ___
2.		about ___
3.		about ___

How long is the yarn? Use the star ruler to measure.

4. ___7___ stars long

5. ___12___ stars long

Getting Ready for Grade 2   thirty-five **GR35**

Write 1, 2, and 3 to measure the strings from **shortest** to **longest**. Then measure with cubes. Write the lengths.

6.
2 ___6___ cubes long
1 ___4___ cubes long
3 ___8___ cubes long

7.
3 ___10___ cubes long
2 ___7___ cubes long
1 ___5___ cubes long

8. Read the clock. Choose the correct time.

- ○ 8:00
- ○ 8:30
- ○ 9:00
- ● 9:30

GR36 thirty-six

---

2 PRACTICE

▶ Share and Show · Guided Practice

- **Where does the hour hand point for time to the hour and time to the half hour?** For time to the hour, the hour hand points to the number. At time to the half hour, the hour hand points halfway between two numbers.

Have children complete Exercises 1–3.

Use **Math Talk** to disccuss with children the placement of the hour hand at half past an hour.

▶ On Your Own

If children complete Exercises 1–3 correctly, assign Exercises 4–9.

- **What is the time in Exercise 6?** 11:30 **What is the time in Exercise 7?** 11:00

▶ Problem Solving

UNLOCK THE PROBLEM For Exercise 10, children draw clock hands to show time at the half hour.

- **Is the time Liam has soccer practice a time to the hour or the half hour? How do you know?** time to the half hour; Possible answer: half past 10:00 names a time to the half hour.

3 SUMMARIZE

Math Processes and Practices

Essential Question

How do you tell time to the hour and half hour on an analog clock? I look at the hour hand. On the hour, it points to the hour. On the half hour, it points halfway between the hour number and the next hour number. The minute hand points to 12 on the hour and to 6 on the half hour.

Math Journal WRITE Math

Draw a clock with an hour hand and a minute hand. Show the time 3:00.

LESSON 16

Use a Picture Graph

LESSON AT A GLANCE

Lesson Objective
Read and interpret information displayed on a picture graph.

Essential Question
How do you read a picture graph?

Materials
MathBoard

GO DIGITAL
⌐ Animated Math Models
MM HMH Mega Math

1 TEACH and TALK 🖥️ • Animated Math Models

▶ **Model and Draw** `Math Processes and Practices`

Read aloud the title and labels on the graph.

• **What does this picture graph show?** whether children chose mustard or ketchup

• **How many children chose mustard or ketchup?** 8 **How do you know?** Each stick person stands for 1 child, and there are 8 stick people.

• **How many children chose mustard?** 3 **How do you know?** I count the stick people in the row labeled "mustard."

2 PRACTICE 🖊️MATH BOARD

▶ **Share and Show** • Guided Practice

• **What does this picture graph show?** whether children are wearing black, white, or blue socks

Have children complete Exercises 1–3.

Use Math Talk to ensure children understand how to read a picture graph.

PG82 Planning Guide

This lesson builds on picture graphs presented in Chapter 10 and prepares children for using graphs taught in Grade 2.

Name _____

Use a Picture Graph
Essential Question How do you read a picture graph?

Model and Draw

Our Favorite Hot Dog Toppings

🫙 mustard	👤	👤	👤		
🍾 ketchup	👤	👤	👤	👤	👤

Each 👤 stands for 1 child.

_3_ children chose 🫙.

Most children chose _ketchup_.

_2_ fewer children chose 🫙 than 🍾.

Share and Show 🖊️MATH BOARD

Our Sock Colors

🧦 black	👤	👤			
🧦 white	👤	👤	👤	👤	👤
🧦 blue	👤	👤	👤		

Each 👤 stands for 1 child.

Use the picture graph to answer the questions.

1. How many children are wearing 🧦? _3_

2. What color of socks are most of the children wearing? _white_

3. How many more children wear 🧦 than 🧦? _4_

Possible answer: I counted back to find the difference between 6 and 2.

Math Talk How did you find the answer to Exercise 3?

© Houghton Mifflin Harcourt Publishing Company

Getting Ready for Grade 2   thirty-seven **GR37**

GR: Practice, p. GRP16

Name _____   Lesson 16
Use a Picture Graph

Lassie's Day

🐕 play	⏰	⏰	⏰			
🐕 eat	⏰	⏰				
🐕 rest	⏰	⏰	⏰	⏰	⏰	⏰

Each ⏰ stands for 1 hour.

Use the picture graph to answer each question.

1. What did Lassie do most of the day? Circle.
[image] [image] [image]

2. How many hours did Lassie 🐕 today? _4_ hours

3. How many more hours did Lassie spend 🐕 than 🐕? _3_ hours

4. How many hours did Lassie 🐕 and 🐕? _7_ hours

Problem Solving Real World

5. Yesterday Lassie spent 2 hours 🐕. How many more hours did Lassie spend 🐕 today? _2_ hours

Getting Ready for Grade 2   sixteen **GRP16**

GR: Reteach, p. GRR16

Name _____   Lesson 16
Reteach
Use a Picture Graph

Grapes We Like

🍇 green grapes	👤	👤	👤	👤
🍇 purple grapes	👤	👤		

Each 👤 stands for 1 child.

How many children chose 🍇?
Count the 👤 in the row.
_5_ children

Which grapes did fewer children chose?
THINK
Which row has fewer 👤?
purple grapes

Our Shirt Colors

👕 red	👤	👤		
👕 yellow	👤	👤	👤	
👕 blue	👤	👤	👤	👤

Each 👤 stands for 1 child.

Use the picture graph to answer the questions.

1. How many children are there in all? _11_ children

2. How many children are wearing 👕? _2_ children

3. What color shirts are most of the children wearing? _blue_

4. How many more children are wearing 👕 than 👕? _2_ children

Reteach   GRR16   Grade 1

---

*GR – Getting Ready Lessons and Resources (*www.thinkcentral.com*)

On Your Own

Our Weather

rainy	◯	◯	◯	◯		
sunny	◯	◯				
cloudy	◯	◯	◯	◯	◯	◯

Each ◯ stands for I day.

Use the picture graph to answer each question.

4. How many days in all are shown on the graph?

   __12__ days

5. What was the weather for most days? Circle.

6. How many fewer days were than ☀?

   __2__ days

7. How many ☀ and ☀ days were there?

   __8__ days

Problem Solving

8. Today is sunny. Robin puts one more ☀ on the graph. How many ☀ days are there now?

   __3__ days

 TAKE HOME ACTIVITY • Help your child make a picture graph to show the eye color of 10 friends and family members.

GR38 thirty-eight

On Your Own

If children complete Exercises 1–3 correctly, assign Exercises 4–7. Children will need to read the picture graph, answer questions about the data, and make comparisons.

- **How do you compare three rows on a picture graph?** I look to see which row has more. I can count to see how many more or how many fewer.

Problem Solving

UNLOCK THE PROBLEM In order to solve the problem in Exercise 8, children will need to refer to the graph at the top of the page.

- **What do you need to find on the picture graph in order to solve the problem?** I need to find how many sunny days are already shown on the picture graph.

3 SUMMARIZE

Math Processes and Practices

Essential Question

How do you read a picture graph? I can see how many pieces of data are recorded and how many are in each category. I can see which category has more or less, and I can find how many more or less.

Math Journal   WRITE Math

Look at the picture graph, Our Weather. Write a different question that can be answered by reading the graph.

Use a Bar Graph

LESSON AT A GLANCE

Lesson Objective
Read and interpret information displayed on a bar graph.

Essential Question
How do you read a bar graph?

Materials
MathBoard

☑ Animated Math Models

〽〽 HMH Mega Math

1 TEACH and TALK 〈GO DIGITAL〉 • Animated Math Models

▶ **Model and Draw** [Math Processes and Practices]

Read aloud the title and labels on the graph.

- **What does this bar graph show?** the number of goldfish, guppies, and angel fish in the class aquarium
- **How is a bar graph different from a picture graph?** A bar graph has numbers at the bottom, and it has bars instead of pictures.

2 PRACTICE 〈MATH BOARD〉

▶ **Share and Show** • Guided Practice

- **How do you tell the number of fish by looking at a bar?** You read the number below the end of the bar.
- **How do you compare data on the graph?** You compare the lengths of the bars or the numbers the bars show.

Have children complete Exercises 1–4.

Use Math Talk to check children's understanding of how to read a bar graph.

This lesson builds on bar graphs presented in Chapter 10 and prepares children for using graphs taught in Grade 2.

Name _____

Use a Bar Graph
Essential Question How do you read a bar graph?

〈 Model and Draw 〉

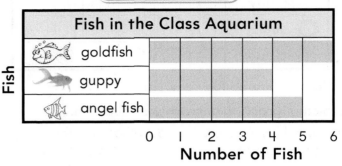

Fish in the Class Aquarium

(Fish: goldfish, guppy, angel fish — Number of Fish: 0 1 2 3 4 5 6)

To find how many, read the number below the end of the bar.

__6__ fish are 🐟.

〈 Share and Show 〉 〈MATH BOARD〉

Use the bar graph to answer the questions.

1. How many fish are in the aquarium?

__15__ fish

2. How many fish in the aquarium are ?

__5__ fish

3. How many fewer fish are 🐟 than 🐟?

__2__ fish

4. Are more of the fish 🐟 or 🐟?

__goldfish__

Possible answer: I added 6 + 4 + 5.

 Math Talk How did you find the answer for Exercise 1?

Getting Ready for Grade 2

thirty-nine **GR39**

GR: Practice, p. GRP17

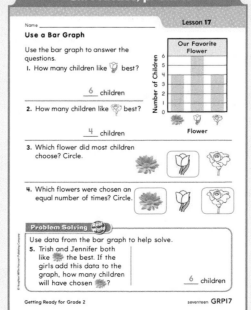

Name _____   Lesson 17

Use a Bar Graph

Use the bar graph to answer the questions.

Our Favorite Flower

1. How many children like 🌼 best?

__6__ children

2. How many children like 🌸 best?

__4__ children

3. Which flower did most children choose? Circle.

4. Which flowers were chosen an equal number of times? Circle.

〈 Problem Solving 〉

Use data from the bar graph to help solve.

5. Trish and Jennifer both like 🌸 the best. If the girls add this data to the graph, how many children will have chosen 🌸?

__6__ children

Getting Ready for Grade 2   seventeen **GRP17**

GR: Reteach, p. GRR17

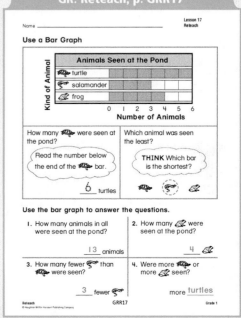

Name _____   Lesson 17 Reteach

Use a Bar Graph

Animals Seen at the Pond

(Kind of Animal: turtle, salamander, frog — Number of Animals: 0 1 2 3 4 5 6)

How many 🐢 were seen at the pond?

Read the number below the end of the 🐢 bar.

__6__ turtles

Which animal was seen the least?

THINK Which bar is the shortest?

Use the bar graph to answer the questions.

1. How many animals in all were seen at the pond?

__13__ animals

2. How many 🐸 were seen at the pond?

__4__ 🐸

3. How many fewer 🐸 than 🐢 were seen?

__3__ fewer 🐸

4. Were more 🐸 or more 🐢 seen?

more __turtles__

Reteach   **GRR17**   Grade 1

---

*GR – Getting Ready Lessons and Resources (www.thinkcentral.com)

On Your Own

Use the bar graph to answer the questions.

5. How many children chose ?

_____3_____ children

6. How many children chose ?

_____4_____ children

7. Which vegetable did most children choose? Circle.

8. Which vegetables were chosen the same number of times? Circle.

Our Favorite Vegetables

Number of Children

```
5
4  ▓        ▓
3  ▓   ▓    ▓
2  ▓   ▓    ▓
1  ▓   ▓    ▓
0  ▓   ▓    ▓
  carrots potatoes corn
```

Kinds of Vegetables

Problem Solving *Real World*

Use the bar graph to solve.

9. Brad and Glen both like corn the best. If the boys add this to the graph, how many children will have chosen corn?

_____5_____ children

 **TAKE HOME ACTIVITY** • Ask your child to decide whether they prefer carrots or potatoes. Then have your child color to add their choice to the bar graph on this page.

GR40 forty

© Houghton Mifflin Harcourt Publishing Company

▶ **On Your Own**

If children complete Exercises 1–4 correctly, assign Exercises 5–8. To complete the exercises, children will need to use the bar graph at the top of the page.

• **What does this bar graph show?** how many children prefer carrots, potatoes, or corn

▶ **Problem Solving**

UNLOCK THE PROBLEM Children can solve the problem in Exercise 9 by using the bar graph.

• **What do you need to find on the bar graph in order to solve the problem?** I need to find how many children chose corn.

3 SUMMARIZE

Math Processes and Practices

Essential Question

How do you read a bar graph? Possible answer: I can see how many are in each category. I can see which category has more or less, and I can find how many more or less.

Math Journal WRITE Math

Look at the bar graph, Our Favorite Vegetables. Write a different question that can be answered by reading the graph.

LESSON 18

Take a Survey

LESSON AT A GLANCE

Lesson Objective
Take a survey and record the results.

Essential Question
How can you take a survey?

Vocabulary
survey

Materials
MathBoard

☑ Animated Math Models

---

1 TEACH and TALK • Animated Math Models

▶ **Model and Draw** (Math Processes and Practices)

Review tally charts by having children tell what they are.

- **What does this tally chart show?** Jane's friends' favorite wild animals; 5 of Jane's friends chose elephants, 3 chose monkeys, and 2 chose tigers.

- **How do you think Jane took this survey?** Possible answer: She chose three wild animals and asked each of 10 friends to name their favorite of the three wild animals. Then Jane recorded her friends' answers in a tally chart.

---

2 PRACTICE

▶ **Share and Show** • Guided Practice

Before children take their surveys, remind them to ask 10 classmates which wild animal is their favorite. Have them record the choices in the tally chart.

- **Will any children choose lions? Why or why not?** No, because the tally chart on this page does not list lion as a choice.

This lesson builds on reading tally charts presented in Chapter 9 and prepares children for interpreting data collected from surveys taught in Grade 2.

Name _____

Take a Survey
Essential Question How can you take a survey?

Model and Draw

You can take a **survey** to get information. Jane took a survey of her friends' favorite wild animals. The tally chart shows the results.

REMEMBER Each tally mark stands for one friend's choice.

Favorite Wild Animal	
Animal	Tally
elephant	卌
monkey	III
tiger	II

Share and Show

1. Take a survey. Check children's work.
   Ask 10 classmates which wild animal is their favorite. Use tally marks to show their answers.
   For 2–4, answers should reflect data represented in tally charts.

Our Favorite Wild Animal	
Animal	Tally
elephant	
monkey	
tiger	

2. How many children did not choose tiger?
   _____ children

3. Did more children choose elephant or tiger? _____

4. The most children chose _____ as their favorite. Possible answer: I could take a survey of favorite art projects with choices drawing, painting, and clay.

 Math Talk Describe a different survey that you could take. What would the choices be?

Getting Ready for Grade 2   forty-one **GR41**

© Houghton Mifflin Harcourt Publishing Company

GR: Practice, p. GRP18

Name _____   Lesson 18
Take a Survey

1. Take a survey. Ask 10 classmates which fruit is their favorite. Use tally marks to show their answers.
Check children's work.
Exercises 2–5 should reflect data recorded in the chart.

Our Favorite Fruit	
Fruit	Tally
apple	
banana	
orange	

2. Which fruit did the fewest classmates choose? _____

3. Which fruit did the most classmates choose? _____

4. Did more classmates choose apple or orange? _____

5. _____ classmates chose a fruit that was not apple.

Problem Solving (Real World)

6. Felix wants to ask 12 friends which pet is their favorite. He makes 1 tally mark for each child's answer. How many more friends does he need to ask?

Our Favorite Pets	
Pet	Tally
dog	卌
cat	III
bird	I

____3____ more friends

Getting Ready for Grade 2   eighteen **GRP18**

GR: Reteach, p. GRR18

Name _____   Lesson 18
                                   Reteach
Take a Survey

When you take a survey, you collect information. Tally marks help you keep track of the information you collect.

Chris took a survey of his friends' favorite lunch. The tally chart shows their answers.

__3__ children chose sandwich.
__6__ children chose pizza.
__1__ child chose salad.

Our Favorite Lunch	
Lunch	Tally
sandwich	III
pizza	卌 I
salad	I

The most children chose ____pizza____.

Check children's work.
1. Take a survey.
   Ask 10 classmates which lunch is their favorite. Use tally marks to show their answers.

Our Favorite Lunch	
Lunch	Tally
sandwich	
pizza	
salad	
taco	

2. Did more children choose pizza or taco? _____

3. The most children chose _____

Reteach   GRR18   Grade 1

*****GR** – Getting Ready Lessons and Resources (*www.thinkcentral.com*)

On Your Own

5. Take a survey. Ask 10 classmates which color is their favorite. Use tally marks to show their answers.

Our Favorite Color	
Color	Tally
red	
blue	
green	

Check children's work.

For 6–10, answers should reflect data recorded in the chart.

6. Which color was chosen by the fewest classmates? _____

7. Which color did the most classmates choose? _____

8. Did more classmates choose red or green? _____

9. _____ classmates chose a color that was not red.

10. Did fewer children choose blue or green? _____

Problem Solving Real World

11. Jeff wants to ask 10 classmates which snack is their favorite. He makes 1 tally mark for each child's answer. How many more classmates does he need to ask?

Our Favorite Snack	
Snack	Tally
pretzels	II
apples	I
popcorn	ᕼᕼ

____2____ more classmates

TAKE HOME ACTIVITY • Have your child survey family members about their favorite sport and make a tally chart to show the results.

GR42 forty-two

Have children complete Exercises 1–4.

Use Math Talk to encourage children to suggest possible surveys, such as favorite school subjects or favorite books. Discuss possible choices for each survey.

▶ **On Your Own**

If children completed Exercises 1–4 correctly, assign Exercises 5–10.

Point out the three color choices shown in the tally chart. Have a volunteer suggest a survey question to ask about favorite colors. Have children take the survey and record the data in the tally chart. Children then use the tally chart to answer Exercises 6–10.

- **How can you check to make sure that you asked 10 classmates to answer your survey question?** Possible answer: I can count the total number of tally marks to be sure there are 10 in all.

▶ **Problem Solving** Real World

UNLOCK THE PROBLEM Exercise 11 requires children to model with mathematics to find the total number of tallies already in the chart and then subtract that number from 10.

- **What is the first step you will do to solve this problem?** Count the number of tally marks there are so far in the tally chart.

- **What is the next step you will do?** Subtract the number from 10 to find how many more classmates need to be surveyed to have 10 in all.

Have volunteers suggest a question that can be answered by using the information in the tally chart. Then use the chart to answer the question.

3 SUMMARIZE

Math Processes and Practices

Essential Question

How can you take a survey? Possible answer: I can make up a survey question with some choices. I can ask a number of people the question. Then I can record their answers next to each choice, using tally marks in a tally chart.

Math Journal  WRITE Math

Make a tally chart to show that 7 children like the color green and 4 children like the color purple.

LESSON 19

Identify Shapes

LESSON AT A GLANCE

Lesson Objective
Use attributes to help identify two-dimensional shapes.

Essential Question
How can attributes help you identify a shape?

Materials
MathBoard

GO DIGITAL
- Animated Math Models
- HMH Mega Math

---

1 TEACH and TALK [GO DIGITAL] • Animated Math Models

▶ Model and Draw [Math Processes and Practices]

Use the small diagram to review the terms *side* and *vertex*. Then discuss these attributes.

- **How can sides and vertices help you identify a hexagon?** I can count to see if there are 6 sides and 6 vertices.

- **Can you always identify the shape by counting the sides and vertices? Explain.** No. Possible answer: A shape with 4 sides and 4 vertices might be a square, rectangle, or trapezoid. It depends on how long the sides are and if they are slanted.

2 PRACTICE [MATH BOARD]

▶ Share and Show • Guided Practice

- **How are the first two shapes in Exercise 1 alike?** They both have 3 sides, 3 vertices, and the same shape name.

Have children complete Exercises 1–4.

Use Math Talk to have children compare attributes of a square and a non-square rectangle.

This lesson builds on identifying shapes presented in Chapter 11 and prepares children for further work with attributes in Grade 2.

Name _____

Identify Shapes

Essential Question How can attributes help you identify a shape?

Model and Draw

The number of sides and vertices help you identify a shape.

 ← vertex ← side

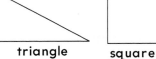

triangle   square   rectangle   trapezoid   hexagon

3 sides, 3 vertices   4 sides, 4 vertices   6 sides, 6 vertices

Share and Show [MATH BOARD]

Circle to answer the question. Write to name the shape.

1. Which shape has 4 sides?

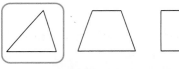

square

2. Which shape has 3 vertices?

triangle

3. Which shape has 6 sides?

hexagon

4. Which shape has 4 vertices?

trapezoid

Possible answer: They both have 4 sides and 4 vertices.

Math Talk How are a square and a rectangle alike?

Getting Ready for Grade 2   forty-three **GR43**

GR: Practice, p. GRP19

Name _____   **Lesson 19**

Identify Shapes

Circle to answer the question. Write to name.

1. Which shape has 4 vertices?

triangle   hexagon   trapezoid
trapezoid

2. Which shape has 4 sides?

rectangle   hexagon   triangle
rectangle

3. Which shape has 6 sides?

triangle   hexagon   square
hexagon

4. Which shape has 3 vertices?

rectangle   triangle   trapezoid
triangle

Problem Solving [Real World]

5. Mira, Liz, and Devin all draw shapes with 4 vertices. Their shapes look different and have different names. Draw 3 shapes the children might have drawn. Label each shape with its shape name.

rectangle   square   trapezoid

Getting Ready for Grade 2   nineteen **GRP19**

GR: Reteach, p. GRR19

Name _____   Lesson 19 Reteach

Identify Shapes

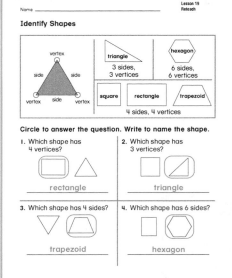

vertex   triangle   hexagon
3 sides, 3 vertices   6 sides, 6 vertices

side   side

vertex   side   vertex   square   rectangle   trapezoid

4 sides, 4 vertices

Circle to answer the question. Write to name the shape.

1. Which shape has 4 vertices?

rectangle

2. Which shape has 3 vertices?

triangle

3. Which shape has 4 sides?

trapezoid

4. Which shape has 6 sides?

hexagon

Reteach   GRR19   Grade 1

***GR** – Getting Ready Lessons and Resources (www.thinkcentral.com)*

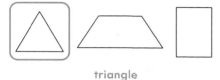

Circle to answer the question. Write to name the shape.

5. Which shape has 3 sides?

_____ triangle

6. Which shape has 4 vertices?

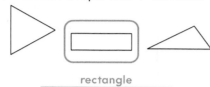

_____ rectangle

7. Which shape has 4 sides?

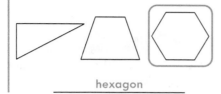

_____ square

8. Which shape has 6 vertices?

_____ hexagon

Problem Solving Real World

9. Jason, Mat, and Carrie each draw a shape with 4 sides. The shapes look different and have different names.

Draw 3 shapes the children might have drawn. Write to name each shape. Possible answers:

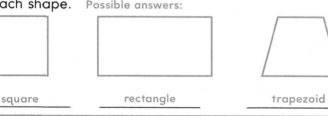

_____ square   _____ rectangle   _____ trapezoid

 TAKE HOME ACTIVITY • Have your child look around the house to find something that looks like a rectangle. Then have your child point to the rectangle and count the vertices. Repeat with the sides.

GR44 forty-four

© Houghton Mifflin Harcourt Publishing Company

▶ **On Your Own**

If children complete Exercises 1–4 correctly, have them continue to use defining attributes to identify the shapes in Exercises 5–8.

• **What is the first shape in Exercise 5?** triangle **What is the first shape in Exercise 6?** triangle **Why do the two triangles look different?** Possible answer: They are turned in different directions.

▶ **Problem Solving** Real World

UNLOCK THE PROBLEM Read aloud the problem in Exercise 9. Then have children draw to show a possible scenario.

• **What do the children's shapes have in common?** They all have 4 sides.

• **How might the shapes be different?** The sides might be different lengths. A shape might have some slanted sides.

3 SUMMARIZE

Math Processes and Practices

Essential Question

How can attributes help you identify a shape? If I know how many sides or vertices a shape has, it helps me identify what shape it is.

Math Journal WRITE Math

Draw a square. Write to describe its attributes.

LESSON 20

Equal Shares

LESSON AT A GLANCE

Lesson Objective
Identify halves and fourths in circles and rectangles.

Essential Question
How can you name two or four equal shares?

Materials
MathBoard

GO DIGITAL
- Animated Math Models
- HMH Mega Math

1 TEACH and TALK
GO DIGITAL • Animated Math Models

▶ Model and Draw
Math Processes and Practices

Use the illustrations at the top of the page to discuss halves and fourths.

- **A whole rectangle has how many halves?** 2 halves **A whole rectangle has how many fourths?** 4 fourths
- **Can one half of a rectangle be larger than the other half? Explain.** No. If one part is larger, the parts are not halves because halves are equal shares.
- **How could you show that the 4 fourths of the rectangle are equal?** Possible answer: I could cut them apart and stack them to show that they match.

This lesson builds on equal shares presented in Chapter 12 and prepares for further work with equal shares taught in Grade 2.

Name _____

Equal Shares
Essential Question How can you name two or four equal shares?

Model and Draw

| half | half |

| fourth | fourth |
| fourth | fourth |

_2_ equal shares
_2_ halves

_4_ equal shares
_4_ fourths

Share and Show
MATH BOARD

Circle the shape that shows equal shares. Write to name the equal shares.

1. _____ halves

2. _____ halves

3. _____ fourths

4. _____ fourths

Possible answer: No, because half of a circle is not the same size and shape as half of a square.

Math Talk Are all equal shares the same size and shape? Explain.

forty-five **GR45**

GR: Practice, p. GRP20

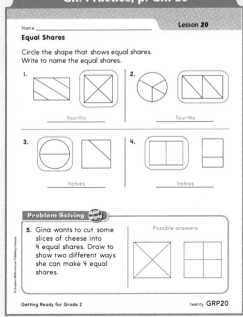

Name _____   Lesson 20
Equal Shares

Circle the shape that shows equal shares. Write to name the equal shares.

1. _____ fourths   2. _____ fourths

3. _____ halves   4. _____ halves

Problem Solving
5. Gina wants to cut some slices of cheese into 4 equal shares. Draw to show two different ways she can make 4 equal shares.

Possible answers:

Getting Ready for Grade 2   twenty GRP20

GR: Reteach, p. GRR20

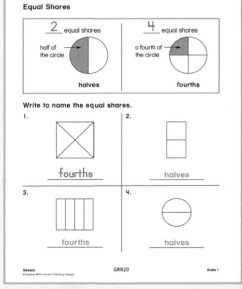

Name _____   Lesson 20 Reteach
Equal Shares

_2_ equal shares   _4_ equal shares
half of the circle   a fourth of the circle
halves   fourths

Write to name the equal shares.

1.   2.
fourths   _halves_

3.   4.
fourths   _halves_

Reteach   GRR20   Grade 1

*GR – Getting Ready Lessons and Resources (*www.thinkcentral.com*)

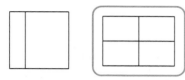

On Your Own

Circle the shape that shows equal shares. Write to name
the equal shares.

5.

fourths

6.

fourths

7.

halves

8.

halves

Problem Solving

9. Riley wants to share his cracker with a friend. Draw to show
two different ways Riley can cut the cracker into equal shares.

Possible answer:

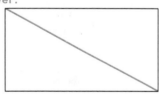

 TAKE HOME ACTIVITY • Ask your child to help you cut a piece of toast into
fourths.

GR46   forty-six

© Houghton Mifflin Harcourt Publishing Company

Getting Ready Lessons and Resources, pp. GR47–GR48   ✓ **Checkpoint**

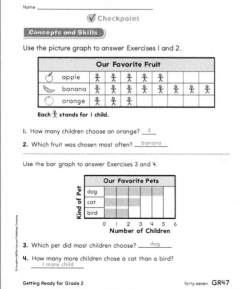

---

② **PRACTICE**

▶ **Share and Show** • Guided Practice

• **Explain how you will know what to circle
in Exercise 1.** Only one square shows equal shares.
I find that square and circle it.

Use **Math Talk** to check children's
understanding of the concept of equal
shares, halves, and fourths.

▶ **On Your Own**

If children complete Exercises 1–4 correctly,
assign Exercises 5–8.

• **What will you look for when you are
trying to identify a shape that shows
fourths?** Possible answer: 4 equal-sized parts

• **What will you look for when you are
trying to identify a shape that shows
halves?** Possible answer: 2 equal-sized parts

▶ **Problem Solving**

UNLOCK THE PROBLEM Read aloud the
problem in Exercise 9. Children can refer
to the illustrations in Exercises 5–8 for
partitioning ideas.

• **How many equal shares will you cut each
cracker into?** Possible answer: 2 equal shares,
because I share with one friend.

③ **SUMMARIZE**

Math Processes and Practices

Essential Question

**How can you name two or four equal
shares?** If a shape shows 2 equal shares, it is halves.
If it shows 4 equal shares, it is fourths.

Math Journal  Math

Draw two circles. Draw to show 2 equal
shares in one circle. Draw to show 4 equal
shares in the other. Write halves or fourths
to name the equal shares.

Getting Ready for Grade 2
Test
LESSONS 12 TO 20

Summative Assessment

Use the **Getting Ready Test** to assess children's progress in Getting Ready for Grade 2 Lessons 12–20.

Getting Ready Tests are provided in multiple-choice and mixed-response format in the *Getting Ready Lessons and Resources*.

GO DIGITAL Getting Ready Test is available online.

Name _____

Getting Ready Test
Lessons 12–20
Page 1

Choose the correct answer.

1. Use the paper clip ruler to measure.

   How long is the yarn?
   - about 6 🔗
   - about 5 🔗
   - ● about 4 🔗
   - about 3 🔗

2. The clock shows when Macy wakes up.

   What time is it?
   - 7:00
   - ● 8:00
   - 7:30
   - 12:00

3. Which shape shows 2 equal shares?
   - ○ (circle)
   - ○ (circle with vertical line)
   - ○ (circle)
   - ● (circle with horizontal line)

4. Ellen uses 🔗 to measure the length of an object. Which object did she measure?
   - a bed
   - ● a stapler
   - a door
   - a printer

Assessment Guide
© Houghton Mifflin Harcourt Publishing Company
GRT7
Mixed Response

Name _____

Getting Ready Test
Lessons 12–20
Page 2

5. Which yarn is the **longest**?
   - ○ ——
   - ○ ———
   - ● ————
   - ○ ——

6. Use the tally chart to answer the question.

Favorite Lunches	
Food	**Tally**
Salad	III
Pizza	IIII
Sandwich	II

   How many children chose pizza?
   - ○ 10
   - ○ 3
   - ● 5
   - ○ 2

7. Use the paper clip ruler to measure.

   How long is the stick?
   - about 2 paper clips
   - ● about 3 paper clips
   - about 4 paper clips
   - about 5 paper clips

8. Parker uses a ✏️ to measure an object. Which object did he measure?
   - an eraser
   - a glue stick
   - ● a desk
   - a marker

Assessment Guide
© Houghton Mifflin Harcourt Publishing Company
GRT8
Mixed Response

Name _____

Getting Ready Test
Lessons 12–20
Page 3

9. Use the picture graph to answer the question.

Favorite Fruits	
🍎 apple	👤 👤 👤
🍊 orange	👤 👤 👤 👤 👤

   Each 👤 stands for 1 child.

   How many children chose oranges?
   - ○ 3
   - ○ 5
   - ○ 4
   - ● 6

10. Use the bar graph to answer the question.

    Animals at the Pet Store
    Puppies / Kittens / Hamsters
    0 1 2 3 4 5
    Number of Animals

    How many more puppies than kittens are there?
    - ● 1 more
    - ○ 3 more
    - ○ 2 more
    - ○ 4 more

11. Which shape has 3 sides?
    - ○ (circle)
    - ● (triangle)
    - ○ (square)
    - ○ (hexagon)

12. The clock shows when Zoe gets home.

    What time is it?
    - 3:00
    - 4:00
    - 3:30
    - ● 4:30

Assessment Guide
© Houghton Mifflin Harcourt Publishing Company
GRT9
Mixed Response

Name _____

Getting Ready Test
Lessons 12–20
Page 4

13. Use the tally chart to answer the question.

Our Favorite Drinks	
Drink	**Tally**
Milk	II
Juice	IIII
Water	III

    How many children chose juice?
    - ○ 3
    - ● 5
    - ○ 4
    - ○ 6

14. Which shape has 4 vertices?
    - ● (rectangle)
    - ○ (circle)
    - ○ (triangle)
    - ○ (hexagon)

15. Which string is the **shortest**?
    - ○ ————
    - ○ ———
    - ● ——
    - ○ ————

16. Which shape shows 4 equal shares?
    - ○ (square with 2 parts)
    - ● (square with 4 parts)
    - ○ (square with 3 parts)
    - ○ (square with X)

Assessment Guide
© Houghton Mifflin Harcourt Publishing Company
GRT10
Mixed Response

✓ Data-Driven Decision Making ▲ RtI

Item	Lesson	Common Error	Intervene With
1, 7, 21	13	May not understand how to use a ruler	R—p. GRR13
2, 12, 20	15	May confuse the hour hand and the minute hand on an analog clock	R—p. GRR15
3, 16, 23	20	May not recognize 2 or 4 equal shares	R—p. GRR20
4, 8, 19	12	May not understand how to choose non-standard units to measure	R—p. GRR12
5, 15, 24	14	May confuse the longest and shortest lengths	R—p. GRR14
6, 13	18	May not understand how to count tally marks	R—p. GRR18

Key: R—Getting Ready Lessons and Resources: Reteach

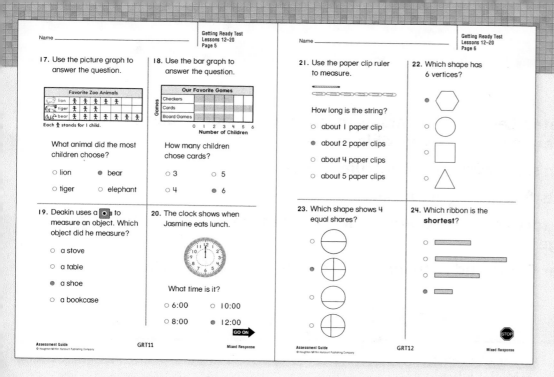

Getting Ready Test
Lessons 12–20
Page 5

Getting Ready Test
Lessons 12–20
Page 6

Portfolio Suggestions The portfolio represents the growth, talents, achievements, and reflections of the mathematics learner. Children might spend a short time selecting work samples for their portfolios.

You may want to have children respond to the following questions:

- Which question was difficult?
- What would you like to learn more about?

For information about how to organize, share, and evaluate portfolios, see the *Chapter Resources*.

✓ Data-Driven Decision Making ▲ RtI

Item	Lesson	Common Error	Intervene With
9, 17	16	May not understand how to find information on a picture graph	R—p. GRR16
10, 18	17	May look at the wrong bars on the graph for information	R—p. GRR17
11, 14, 22	19	May confuse attributes of plane shapes	R—p. GRR19

Key: R—Getting Ready Lessons and Resources: Reteach

Differentiated Centers Kit

The Grab-and-Go!™ Differentiated Centers Kit contains ready-to-use readers, games, and math center activities that are designed for flexible usage.

- Readers that integrate math skills with cross-curricular content.
- Games that engage students to practice math skills.
- Math Center Activities that focus on computation, mental math, geometry, measurement, and challenge activities.

See the Grab-and-Go!™ Teacher Guide and Activity Resources for more information.

Chapter	Grade 1		
1 Addition Concepts	Reader	The Class Party Math Club Join Us Busy Bugs	
	Game	Addition Bingo	
	Activity	Activity 3	Sum Sentences Put It Together How Many Ways?
		Activity 7	Back and Forth
2 Subtraction Concepts	Reader	The Class Party Milk for Sale	
	Game	Subtraction Slide	
	Activity	Activity 5	Apples Away Runaway Squares
		Activity 9	Subtract! Picture This
3 Addition Strategies	Reader	Join Us Doubles Fun on the Farm Funny Bunny Hats	
	Game	Ducky Sums Neighborhood Sums	
	Activity	Activity 7	Double Trouble Back and Forth
		Activity 16	Make a Ten to Add Add With Ten The Sum Is the Same

Chapter		Grade 1	
4 Subtraction Strategies	**Reader**	Math Club Miss Bumble's Garden The Class Party	
	Game	Under the Sea	
	Activity	Activity 5	Apples Away Runaway Squares Plus and Minus
		Activity 9	Picture This
5 Addition and Subtraction Relationships	**Reader**	Picture Puzzles Juggling	
	Game	Ducky Sums Related Fact Race Basic Facts Race	
	Activity	Activity 11	Face Facts Any Way You Cut It Problem Solving
		Activity 16	The Sum Is the Same
		Activity 18	The Missing Piece Number Tales
6 Count and Model Numbers	**Reader**	Join Us Strawberries	
	Game	Puddle Hopping Tens and Ones Race	
	Activity	Activity 14	Teen Time Groups of Ten Ten and Up

Math Center Activity Cards:

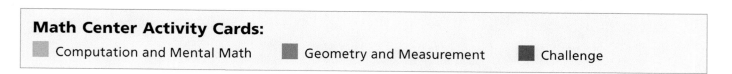

Computation and Mental Math   Geometry and Measurement   Challenge

Chapter		Grade 1	
7 Compare Numbers	**Reader**	Name That Number Strawberries	
	Game	The Greater Game Rainy Day Fun Puddle Hopping	
	Activity	Activity 4	20 Through 50
8 Two-Digit Addition and Subtraction	**Reader**	Garden Party It's a Home Run! Party Plans	
	Game	Neighborhood Sums Flying Along Basic Facts Race	
	Activity	Activity 14	Groups of Ten
		Activity 16	Add With Ten
		Activity 20	Regroup Count On Neat Trick
9 Measurement	**Reader**	The Dog Show Treasure Hunts Time to Play	
	Game	Measure Up! Story Time	
	Activity	Activity 17	Half Past On the Hour

Chapter		Grade 1	
10 Represent Data	Reader	Miss B's Class Makes Tables and Graphs	
	Game	Graph Game	
	Activity	Activity 6	Tally Ho! Graph Math Picture Perfect
		Activity 8	Pass the Bar
11 Three-Dimensional Geometry	Reader	April's First Word Building a Mini-Park	
	Game	On the Water	
	Activity	Activity 10	On the Corner Building Blocks
12 Two-Dimensional Geometry	Reader	Signs Shape Up	
	Game	On the Water	
	Activity	Activity 10	More Alike Than Not On the Corner Building Blocks
		Activity 19	Half Math

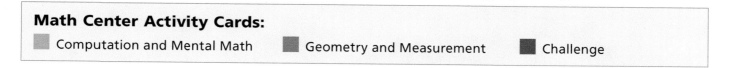

Math Center Activity Cards:
Computation and Mental Math   Geometry and Measurement   Challenge

Sequence Options

Go Math! provides the flexibility to teach the program in a different sequence.
If children need background knowledge for the chapter, use the list of prerequisites.

Chapter	Objectives	Prerequisites
1 Addition Concepts	• Use pictures and concrete objects and the strategy make a model to solve "adding to" and "putting together" addition problems. • Understand, apply, and explore the Additive Identity Property for Addition and the Commutative Property of Addition. • Model and record all the ways to put together numbers within 10. • Build fluency for addition within 10.	
2 Subtraction Concepts	• Use pictures and concrete objects and the strategy make a model to solve "taking from" and "taking apart" subtraction problems. • Compare pictorial groups to understand subtraction. • Identify how many are left when subtracting all or 0. • Model and compare groups to show the meaning of subtraction. • Model and record all of the ways to take apart numbers within 10. • Build fluency for subtraction within 10.	Chapter 1
3 Addition Strategies	• Understand and apply the Commutative Property of Addition for sums within 20. • Use the following strategies to find sums within 20: count on 1, 2, or 3, doubles, doubles plus 1 and doubles minus 1, or make a ten. • Use doubles to create equivalent but easier sums. • Use a ten frame to add 10 and an addend less than 10. • Understand and apply the Associative Property or Commutative Property of Addition to add three addends. • Solve adding to and putting together situations using the strategy draw a picture.	Chapter 1
4 Subtraction Strategies	• Use the following strategies to find differences within 20: count back 1, 2, or 3, use addition to subtract, or make a ten. • Recall addition facts to subtract numbers within 20. • Subtract by breaking apart to make a ten. • Solve subtraction problem situations using the strategy act it out.	Chapter 2
5 Addition and Subtraction Relationships	• Solve addition and subtraction problem situations using the strategy make a model. • Identify and record related facts within 20 and use them to subtract. • Apply the inverse relationship of addition and subtraction. • Represent equivalent forms of numbers using sums and differences within 20. • Determine if an equation is true or false. • Add and subtract facts within 20 and demonstrate fluency for addition and subtraction within 10.	Chapters 1–4
6 Count and Model Numbers	• Use models and write to represent equivalent forms of ten and ones through 120. • Use objects, pictures, and numbers to represent numbers (or quantities) to 100. • Solve problems using the strategy make a model. • Count, read, and write numerals to represent a number of 100 to 120 objects.	Chapters 1–5

Chapter	Objectives	Prerequisites
7 Compare Numbers	• Model and compare two-digit numbers using symbols. • Solve problems using the strategy make a model. • Identify numbers that are 10 less or 10 more than a given number.	Chapter 6
8 Two-Digit Addition and Subtraction	• Add and subtract within 20. • Use and draw models and manipulatives to add two-digit numbers. • Solve and explain two-digit addition word problems using the strategy draw a picture.	Chapters 1–6
9 Measurement	• Order objects by length. • Use the Transitivity Principle to measure indirectly. • Make a nonstandard measuring tool to measure length. • Solve measurement problems using the strategy act it out. • Tell times and write times to the hour and half hour.	Chapter 7
10 Represent Data	• Analyze and compare data shown in a picture graph where each symbol represents one. • Make a picture graph. • Analyze and compare data shown in a bar graph or a tally chart. • Make a bar graph or a tally chart. • Solve problem situations using the strategy make a graph.	Chapter 7
11 Three-Dimensional Geometry	• Identify and describe three-dimensional shapes according to defining attributes. • Compose a new shape by combining three-dimensional shapes. • Use composite three-dimensional shapes to build new shapes. • Identify three-dimensional shapes used to build a composite shape using the strategy act it out. • Identify two-dimensional shapes on three-dimensional shapes.	
12 Two-Dimensional Geometry	• Describe attributes of two-dimensional shapes and use defining attributes to sort shapes. • Compose a new shape by combining two-dimensional shapes. • Make new shapes from composite two-dimensional shapes using the strategy act it out. • Decompose combined shapes into shapes. • Identify equal and unequal parts (or shares) in two-dimensional shapes. • Partition circles and rectangles into two or four equal shares.	Chapter 11

Student Edition Glossary

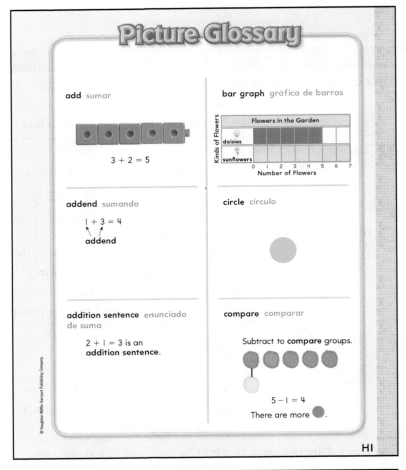

Picture Glossary

add sumar

$3 + 2 = 5$

addend sumando

$1 + 3 = 4$

addend

addition sentence enunciado de suma

$2 + 1 = 3$ is an **addition sentence**.

bar graph gráfica de barras

Flowers in the Garden

Kinds of Flowers
daisies
sunflowers

Number of Flowers
0 1 2 3 4 5 6 7

circle círculo

compare comparar

Subtract to **compare** groups.

$5 - 1 = 4$

There are more

H1

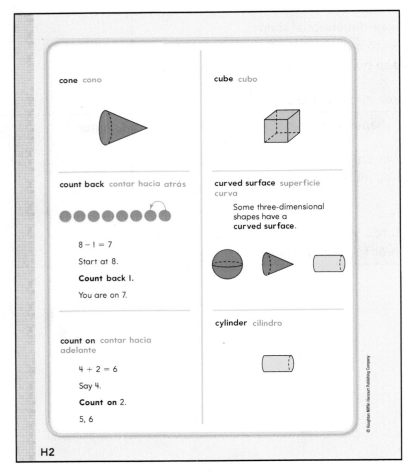

cone cono

count back contar hacia atrás

$8 - 1 = 7$

Start at 8.

Count back 1.

You are on 7.

count on contar hacia adelante

$4 + 2 = 6$

Say 4.

Count on 2.

5, 6

cube cubo

curved surface superficie curva

Some three-dimensional shapes have a **curved surface**.

cylinder cilindro

H2

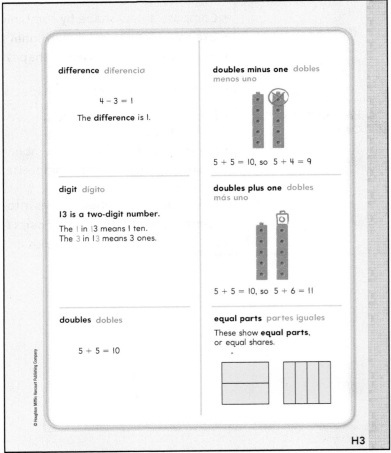

difference diferencia

$4 - 3 = 1$

The **difference** is 1.

digit dígito

13 is a two-digit number.

The 1 in 13 means 1 ten.
The 3 in 13 means 3 ones.

doubles dobles

$5 + 5 = 10$

doubles minus one dobles menos uno

$5 + 5 = 10$, so $5 + 4 = 9$

doubles plus one dobles más uno

$5 + 5 = 10$, so $5 + 6 = 11$

equal parts partes iguales

These show **equal parts**, or equal shares.

H3

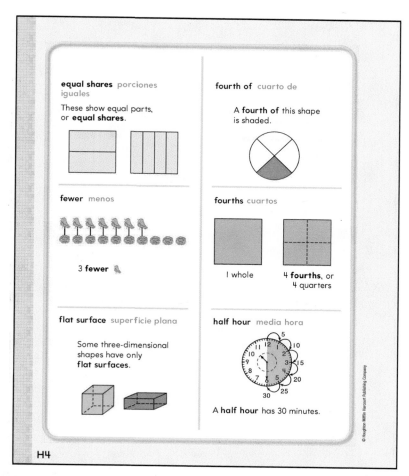

equal shares porciones iguales

These show equal parts, or **equal shares**.

fewer menos

3 **fewer** 🐦

flat surface superficie plana

Some three-dimensional shapes have only **flat surfaces**.

fourth of cuarto de

A **fourth of** this shape is shaded.

fourths cuartos

I whole   4 **fourths**, or 4 quarters

half hour media hora

A **half hour** has 30 minutes.

H4

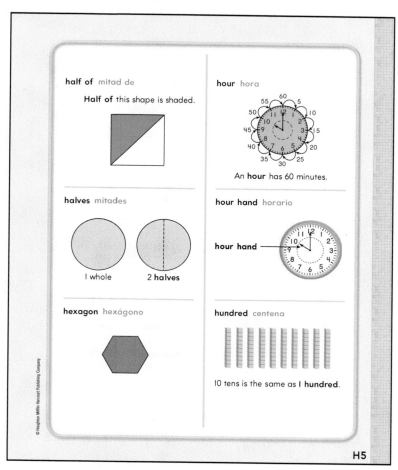

half of mitad de

Half of this shape is shaded.

halves mitades

I whole   2 halves

hexagon hexágono

hour hora

An **hour** has 60 minutes.

hour hand horario

hour hand

hundred centena

10 tens is the same as I **hundred**.

H5

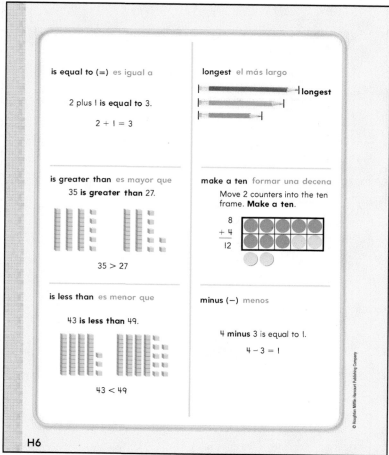

is equal to (=) es igual a

2 plus I is equal to 3.

$2 + 1 = 3$

is greater than es mayor que

35 **is greater than** 27.

$35 > 27$

is less than es menor que

43 **is less than** 49.

$43 < 49$

longest el más largo

longest

make a ten formar una decena

Move 2 counters into the ten frame. **Make a ten.**

$\begin{array}{r} 8 \\ + 4 \\ \hline 12 \end{array}$

minus (−) menos

4 **minus** 3 is equal to 1.

$4 - 3 = 1$

H6

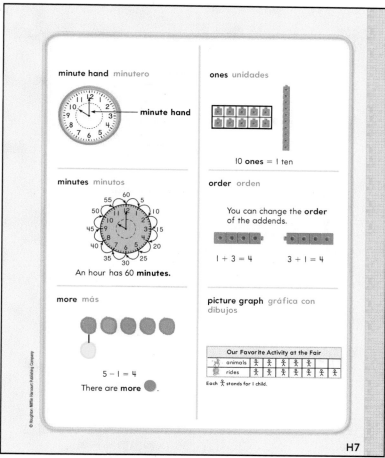

minute hand minutero

minute hand

minutes minutos

An hour has 60 **minutes.**

more más

$5 - 1 = 4$

There are **more** ●.

ones unidades

10 **ones** = 1 ten

order orden

You can change the **order** of the addends.

$1 + 3 = 4$ $3 + 1 = 4$

picture graph gráfica con dibujos

Our Favorite Activity at the Fair						
animals	�§	�§	�§			
rides	�§	�§	�§	�§	�§	�§

Each �§ stands for 1 child.

H7

Student Edition Glossary continued

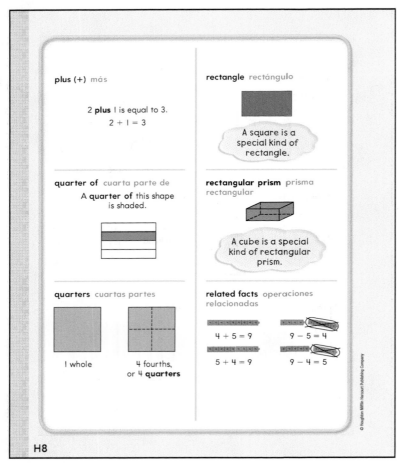

plus (+) más

2 **plus** I is equal to 3.
2 + I = 3

quarter of cuarta parte de
A **quarter of** this shape
is shaded.

quarters cuartas partes

I whole

4 fourths,
or 4 **quarters**

rectangle rectángulo

A square is a
special kind of
rectangle.

rectangular prism prisma
rectangular

A cube is a special
kind of rectangular
prism.

related facts operaciones
relacionadas

4 + 5 = 9   9 − 5 = 4
5 + 4 = 9   9 − 4 = 5

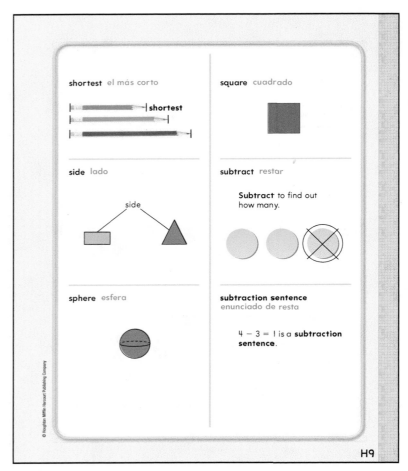

shortest el más corto

shortest

side lado

side

sphere esfera

square cuadrado

subtract restar

Subtract to find out
how many.

subtraction sentence
enunciado de resta

4 − 3 = I is a **subtraction
sentence**.

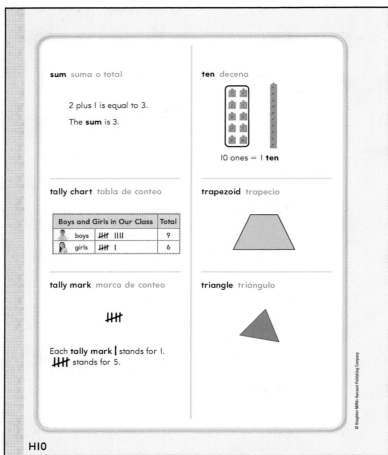

sum suma o total

2 plus I is equal to 3.
The **sum** is 3.

tally chart tabla de conteo

Boys and Girls in Our Class		Total
boys	ЦЖ IIII	9
girls	ЦЖ I	6

tally mark marca de conteo

ЦЖ

Each **tally mark** | stands for I.
ЦЖ stands for 5.

ten decena

10 ones = I **ten**

trapezoid trapecio

triangle triángulo

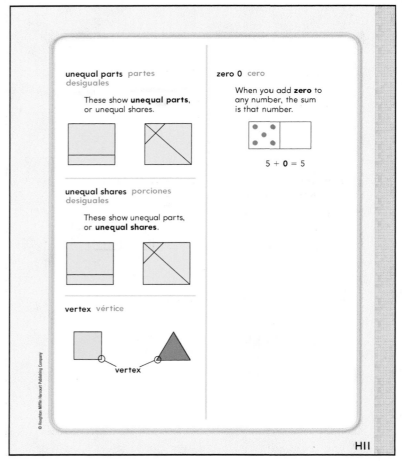

unequal parts partes
desiguales

These show **unequal parts**,
or unequal shares.

unequal shares porciones
desiguales

These show unequal parts,
or **unequal shares**.

vertex vértice

vertex

zero 0 cero

When you add **zero** to
any number, the sum
is that number.

5 + **0** = 5

Teacher Notes

Professional Development References

Bahr, D. L., & de Garcia, L. A. (2010). *Elementary mathematics is anything but elementary.* Belmont, CA: Wadsworth.

Baldi, S., Jin, Y., Skemer, M., Green, P. J., & Herget, D. (2007). *Highlights from PISA 2006: Performance of U.S. 15-year-old students in science and mathematics literacy in an international context* (NCES-2008-016). National Center for Education Statistics, Institute of Education Sciences. Washington, DC: U.S. Department of Education.

Carpenter, T. P., Franke, M. L., & Levi, L. (2003). *Thinking mathematically: Integrating arithmetic and algebra in elementary school.* Portsmouth, NH: Heinemann.

Clements, D. H., & Sarama, J. (2014). *Learning and teaching early math: The learning trajectories approach.* New York: Routledge, Taylor and Francis.

Furhman, S. H., Resnick, L., & Shepard, L. (2009). Standards aren't enough. *Education Week, 29*(7), 28.

Gonzales, P., Williams, T., Jocelyn, L., Roey, S., Katsberg, D., & Brenwald, S. (2008). *Highlights from TIMSS 2007: Mathematics and science achievement of U.S. fourth- and eighth-grade students in an international context* (NCES 2009-001 Revised). National Center for Education Statistics, Institute of Education Sciences. Washington, DC: U.S. Department of Education.

Kennedy, L., Tipps, S., & Johnson, A. (2004). *Guiding children's learning of mathematics* (10th ed.). Belmont, CA: Wadsworth/Thomson Learning.

Marzano, R. J. (2003). *What works in schools: Translating research into action.* Alexandria, VA: ASCD.

National Council of Teachers of Mathematics. (2000). *Principles and standards for school mathematics.* Reston, VA: Author.

National Council of Teachers of Mathematics (2014). *Principles to Actions: Ensuring Mathematical Success for All.* Reston, VA: Author.

National Council of Teachers of Mathematics. (2005). *Standards and Curriculum: A view from the nation, a joint report by the National Council of Teachers of Mathematics (NCTM) and the Association of State Supervisors of Mathematics (ASSM).* J. W. Lott & K. Nishimura (Eds.). Reston, VA: Author.

National Mathematics Advisory Panel. (2008). *Foundations for success: The final report of the National Mathematics Advisory Panel.* Washington, DC: U. S. Department of Education.

National Research Council. (2001). *Adding it up: Helping children learn mathematics.* J. Kilpatrick, J. Swafford, & B. Findell (Eds.). Washington, DC: National Academy Press.

Reed, D. S. (2009). Is there an expectations gap? Educational federalism and the demographic distribution of proficiency cut scores. *American Educational Research Journal, 46*(3), 718-742.

Reys, B. J., Chval, K., Dingman, S., McNaught, M., Regis, T. P., & Togashi, J. (2007). Grade-level learning expectations: A new challenge for elementary mathematics teachers. *Teaching Children Mathematics, 14*(1), 6-11.

Schmoker, M. (2011). *Focus: Elevating the essentials to radically improve student learning.* Alexandria, VA: ASCD.

Schneider, M. (2007). *National Assessment of Education Progress: Mapping 2005 state proficiency standards onto the NAEP scales.* Washington, DC: IES National Center for Education Statistics.

Schwartz, J. E. (2008). *Elementary mathematics pedagogical content knowledge: Powerful ideas for teachers.* Boston, MA: Pearson.

Van de Walle, J. A. (2004). *Elementary and middle school mathematics: Teaching developmentally* (5th ed.). Boston, MA: Pearson.

Van de Walle, J. A. (2007). *Elementary and middle school mathematics: Teaching developmentally* (6th ed.). Boston, MA: Pearson.

Wall, E., & Posamentier, A. (2007). *What successful math teachers do, Grades PreK–5 : 47 research-based strategies for the standards-based classroom.* Thousand Oaks, CA: Corwin Press.

Teacher Notes

Index

About Go Math! Program Overview, *PG4*

About the Math

If Children Ask, 25A, 55A, 69A, 149A, 161A, 197A, 279A, 297A, 361A, 411A, 467A, 531A, 537A, 561A, 581A, 651A, 689A, 695A, 725A

Teaching for Depth, 13A, 19A, 81A, 105A, 137A, 155A, 167A, 185A, 229A, 235A, 255A, 261A, 267A, 303A, 337A, 343A, 385A, 405A, 443A, 479A, 513A, 555A, 575A, 587A, 605A, 639A, 671A, 683A, 719A

Why Teach This, 37A, 43A, 93A, 117A, 131A, 143A, 191A, 211A, 217A, 273A, 309A, 331A, 355A, 367A, 417A, 437A, 455A, 473A, 485A, 549A, 599A, 633A, 677A, 713A

Access Prior Knowledge,

In every Teacher Edition lesson. Some examples are: 13B, 93B, 155B, 217B, 279B, 349B, 411B, 473B, 549B, 611B, 689B, 725B

Act It Out, *241–244, 537–539, 651–654, 695–697*

Activities

Curious George®, Curious About Math with, 9, 65, 127, 207, 251, 327, 395, 433, 509, 571, 629, 667

ELL Language Support, In every Teacher Edition lesson. Some examples are: 13, 25, 285, 417, 581, 683

ELL Vocabulary Activity, See Developing Math Language

Games, *See* Games

Grab-and-Go!™ Differentiated Centers Kit, In every Teacher Edition lesson. Some examples are: 72, 101, 357, 420, 642, 722

Independent Activities, 16, 22, 28, 33, 40, 46, 52, 58, 72, 78, 84, 90, 96, 101, 108, 114, 120, 134, 140, 146, 152, 158, 163, 170, 176, 182, 188, 194, 200, 214, 220, 225, 232, 238, 244, 258, 264, 270, 275, 282, 288, 294, 300, 306, 312, 334, 340, 346, 352, 357, 364, 370, 376, 382, 388, 402, 408, 413, 420, 426, 440, 446, 451, 458, 464, 470, 476, 482, 488, 516, 522, 528, 534, 539, 546, 552, 558, 564, 578, 584, 590, 595, 602, 608, 614, 636, 642, 647, 654, 660, 674, 680, 686, 692, 697, 704, 710, 716, 722, 728

Response to Intervention (RtI), RtI Tier 1 and RtI Tier 2 available online

Take Home Activity, 16, 22, 28, 33, 40, 46, 52, 58, 72, 78, 84, 90, 96, 101, 108, 114, 120, 134, 140, 146, 152, 158, 163, 170, 176, 182, 188, 194, 200, 214, 220, 225, 232, 238, 244, 258, 264, 270, 275, 282, 288, 294, 300, 306, 312, 334, 340, 346, 352, 357, 364, 370, 376, 382, 388, 402, 408, 413, 420, 426, 440, 446, 451, 458, 464, 470, 476, 482, 488, 516, 522, 528, 534, 539, 546, 552, 558, 564, 578, 584, 590, 595, 602, 608, 614, 636, 642, 647, 654, 660, 674, 680, 686, 692, 697, 704, 710, 716, 722, 728

Add, *9H*

Addends, *9H*, 44

identifying, 61

missing addends, *See* unknown addends

order of, 43–46, 131–134

unknown addends, using related facts to find, 261–264, 279–288

Addition

adding to

  model, 19–22, 461–464

  using pictures, 13–16, 55–56

Addition Problem Situations

  Add to/Change Unknown, 9, 16, 32, 62, 217, 248, 256–257, 294, 334, 439–440

  Add to/Result Unknown, 13, 19, 31–37, 40, 55, 62, 127, 134, 137, 140, 143, 146, 170, 197, 199–200, 204, 223, 251, 258, 261, 273, 282, 292, 293–294, 343, 443, 455, 461, 464, 467, 470, 479–481, 485, 498, 590

  Add to/Start Unknown, 257, 420, 488

  Put Together/Addend Unknown, 33, 194, 258, 291, 293, 312, 316, 449, 614

  Put Together/Both Addends Unknown, 15, 134, 146, 182, 258, 420

  Put Together/Total Unknown, 25–28, 34, 62, 131, 134, 149, 167, 179, 185, 191, 194, 198, 199, 200, 293–294, 458, 464, 473, 476, 480–482, 488, 577–578, 584, 589, 600, 606, 611

Teacher Edition and Planning Guide references in *italics*; Planning Guide references begin with PG

Math Journal, *In every Teacher Edition lesson. Some examples are: 16, 72, 420, 476, 660, 722*

Math Processes and Practices
1. Problem Solving. *In many lessons. Some examples are:* 13, 19, 25, 33, 69, 75, 81, 87, 93, 99, 131, 137, 149, 197, 223, 241, 255, 263, 279, 349, 355, 373, 411, 423, 437, 473, 479, 491, 513, 519, 528, 537, 549, 561, 605, 639, 645, 657, 695, 707, 713
2. Abstract and Quantitative Reasoning. *In many lessons. Some examples are:* 69, 75, 81, 87, 93, 99, 167, 169, 173, 179, 197, 229, 241, 255, 285, 309, 337, 349, 367, 385, 417, 443, 445, 467, 473, 481, 485, 525, 531, 549, 555, 599, 639, 645
3. Use and Evaluate Logical Reasoning. *In many lessons. Some examples are:* 163, 187, 191, 217, 241, 291, 343, 349, 423, 437, 449, 485, 491, 513, 519, 531, 537, 575, 581, 587, 593, 599, 605, 611, 639, 645, 713
4. Mathematical Modeling. *In many lessons. Some examples are:* 15, 20, 27, 33, 43, 50, 72, 83, 87, 99, 146, 170, 181, 194, 219, 255, 282, 299, 312, 399, 405, 411, 440, 464, 479, 561, 575, 581, 587, 593, 599, 605, 633, 657, 689, 701, 719
5. Use Mathematical Tools. *In many lessons. Some examples are:* 21, 49, 87, 99, 137, 151, 175, 255, 339, 373, 379, 385, 485, 587, 593, 596, 611, 617, 619
6. Use Precise Mathematical Language. *In many lessons. Some examples are:* 57, 119, 139, 157, 291, 305, 311, 343, 351, 363, 449, 473, 513, 525, 543, 611, 639, 657, 671, 683, 713
7. See Structure. *In many lessons. Some examples are:* 45, 113, 145, 217, 261, 269, 273, 281, 309, 333, 355, 379, 399, 405, 443, 543, 651, 671, 707
8. Generalize. *In many lessons. Some examples are:* 7, 37, 49, 137, 191, 229, 261, 267, 273, 279, 331, 337, 357, 411, 449, 479, 491, 525, 549, 593, 633, 651, 671, 677

Building Math Processes and Practices, 49A, 75A, 179A, 223A, 291A, 379A, 423A, 449A, 519A, 611A, 645A, 707A

Math Processes and Practices, PG18

Math Processes and Practices in Go Math!, PG24

Supporting Math Processes and Practices Through Questioning Strategies, PG23

Teaching for Depth, Math Processes and Practices, 9E, 65E, 127E, 207C, 251E, 327E, 395C, 433E, 509E, 571E, 629C, 667E

Math Talk, In every Student Edition lesson. Some examples are: 13, 25, 367, 385, 707, 725

Measurement
concepts, 509E
length, 509E
    compare and order, 513–516, 519–522
    indirect measurement, 519–522
    nonstandard units, 525–528
time, 543–546, 549–552, 555–558

Mega Math, HMH, *See Technology and Digital Resources*

Mid-Chapter Checkpoint, 34, 102, 164, 226, 276, 358, 414, 452, 540, 596, 648, 698

Minus sign, *65H,* 76, 81–84, 100–101

Minute, *509H,* 555–558

Minute hand, *509H,* 555–558, 562–563

Modalities, *See also specific entries on each B page of every Teacher Edition lesson*
auditory, for example, *14, 70, 268*
kinesthetic, for example, *230, 274, 462, 474*
verbal, for example, *486, 492*
visual, for example, *14, 70, 132, 406*

Model
addition
    adding to, 19–22, 461–464
    addition sentences, 20–22, 25–28, 31–33, 43–46, 50–51
    make a model, 31–33, 255–257
    make a ten to add, *173A,* 173–176, 179–182
    math triangles, *285A,* 285–288
    putting together, 25–28
    tens, 173–176, 179–182
    ways to make numbers to ten, 49–52
    word problems, 31–33, 146, 170, 194, 255–257, 282, 294, 312, 440, 464, 479–482
bar graphs, *571E, 571H, 587A,* 587–590, *593A,* 593–595, 596, 611–614, 617, 619
bar models, *31A,* 31–33, *87A,* 87–90, *99A,* 99–101, 255–258
compare, subtraction, 99–101
numbers in different ways, 373–376, 379–382, 385–388, 485–488
subtraction
    bar models, *87A,* 87–90, *99A,* 99–101, 255–258
    to compare, 99–101
    make a model, 87–90, 99–101, 255–257
    make a ten to subtract, 229–232
    math triangles, *285A,* 285–288
    subtract to compare, *65E, 99A*
    take apart numbers from ten or less, *65E,* 117–120
    taking apart, 81–84
    taking from, 75–78
    tens, 229–232, 449–451
    word problems, 78, 84, 87–90, 220, 241–244, 255–257
tens, 355–357

Models
Compare with Base-Ten Blocks, 399A
Measuring Length with Color Tiles, 525A
Model Using Nets, 657A

Teacher Edition and Planning Guide references in *italics*; Planning Guide references begin with PG